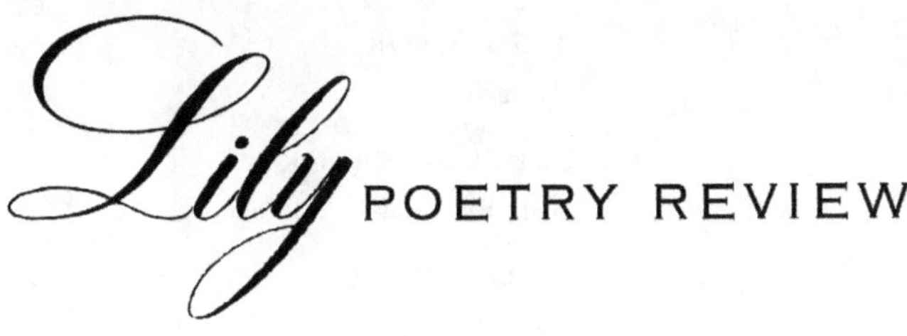

ISSUE 15

❦

GUEST EDITOR

Jennifer Franklin

EDITOR-IN-CHIEF
Eileen Cleary

ASSISTANT EDITOR
Mark Walsh

ART EDITOR
Lisa Sullivan

BOOK REVIEW EDITOR
Amanda Shaw

VISPO EDITOR
Suzanne Mercury

WEB EDITOR
Rebecca Connors

MEDIA AND EVENTS
Frances Donovan

READERS
Susan Kay Anderson, Jules Jacob,
K. T. Landon, Michelle Lynch, Gloria Monaghan,
Tzynya Pinchback, Sarah Dickenson Snyder,
Anastasia Vassos

DESIGN
Martha McCollough

COVER ART, ISSUE 15
Millie Benson, detail, *Vanishing Moon*

TABLE OF CONTENTS

ALICIA OSTRIKER

The Bear's Owner

He will always stand in the street shouting
In the marketplace banging his drum
Banging his drum
The bears will always dance
They will lay their right paw humbly
On his left shoulder
People will always stand around
Or watch from windows
with wonder or laughter
at the master
and the prisoner

FRED MARCHANT

Vigil

Over at last and gone,
the body that was belongs
now to no one, a palpable
absence has unequivocally
arrived, the lack of ambiguity
is breathtaking and you
feel almost grateful for what
loss on this scale might teach,
how quickly you feel a keen
admiration for the literal, how
metaphors make you smile
as they sneak into thought,
seem calculated compared
to the warmth in the hand
you hold until you place it
down gently, thinking gently
does not matter anymore,
you note the bedrail's proud,
embossed medallion, light
from a fluorescent upon it
and on a face that has begun
to look like a mask, you feel
the wish that before the soul
coasts away, it will hover at
the sealed window and signal
you when it is ready to go,
to leave this practical room
that kindness invited you into,
and asked if you would like
a few more minutes alone.

for E.C.M.

FRED MARCHANT

Espalier Pears

Lifted straight from a trained tree limb,

held by those I love, placed in a jewelry

box covered in soft green silk, wrapped

in a taped grocery bag sealed with return

address stickers, off to the post office,

its questions about knives, bombs, liquor,

no none, yes please, a priority overnight

then the plane begins its climb thousands

of feet up and across a night sky, in, out

of clouds, moonlight, then a final approach,

circling the dawn over Winthrop tidal flats,

on time for a morning pickup and delivery,

yellow truck at the gate, now outside our door,

two pears frozen solid from the high altitude,

only yesterday picked from the espaliered tree

whose good arms you trained to be wide open,

and outstretched across the whole continent,

holding on and giving away all at the same time.

for Maxine and Earll Kingston

IAIN HALEY POLLOCK

A Theory Of Arrival (Wetlands)

A host of unnamable winged things
becomes visible in the softening gold
of October day-end. Holy the insects?
Holy the road bisecting the wetland,
vessel for water run down from the hills?
Holy the cars bottlenecked at the signal
turned red? Holy the reeds' silvered heads
rippling slow in the mild wind? All this,
save water and mud, a second coming
or more: an arrival after an arrival after
an arrival. Ragweed and cocklebur,
an arrival. Dragonfly and gypsy moth,
an arrival. Red-winged blackbird flocked
and nested, an arrival. The reeds, their weave
of rhizome and stalk and blade impenetrable,
admitting no vegetal life but their own,
an arrival. A beginning, with each arrival,
a beginning and a collapse and a beginning.
A second coming: a holy that once was not
holy. A second coming or more: reeds
into a landscape of no-reeds until (impenetrable)
reeds become the landscape. Until the birds
that were an arrival before the arrival learn
to braid these blades into nest. Until a blackbird,
red-winged, perches on a stalk, having learned
to spread its avian weight so that the silvered head
does not drop low, remains at the altitude of small
winged things, perches, waits to flash up and arrive
at their flight (a beginning and a collapse and
a beginning). Or else, perches on the stalk height
and lets its song (a holy that was not) tumble
into the landscape (road bisecting a wetland
of second-coming reeds). Into the day-end
that arrives and collapses into October (holy!)
and then will not be October or day-end again.

IAIN HALEY POLLOCK

██ Bells, Tattered ██ #3

STRAPPED TO THE DECK
    of a semi's trailing flatbed,
a load of dug-up propane
    tanks, each blooming
with clods of earth
    from the ground that lately
housed it, float down
    the highway, destined
to sit behind spirals
    of concertina wire,
behind chain link covered
    with corrugated sheets
of blue plastic, to sit
    in the dirt and summer weeds
of the salvage yard, where
    some will be recovered
and refilled with their former
    purpose while others
are emptied, torched apart
    or melted down, and recast
to the rigid proportions
    of some new design.

ON A BLOCK
    of close-in houses,
a blue tarp
    covering the char
& blister at a two-family—
    its abandoned,
flame-gnawed upper stories—
    has come loose
at three corners
    (all but the top right),
& in a spring wind
    that won't let go
of winter, fray-edged
    polyethylene billows out,
threatening to lash
    the kitchen window
next door, before snapping back,
    billowing & snapping
in the recalcitrant cold,
    billowing & snapping
like the untended
    & torn staysail
to a ghost ship rudderless
    in the sea's heavy swell.

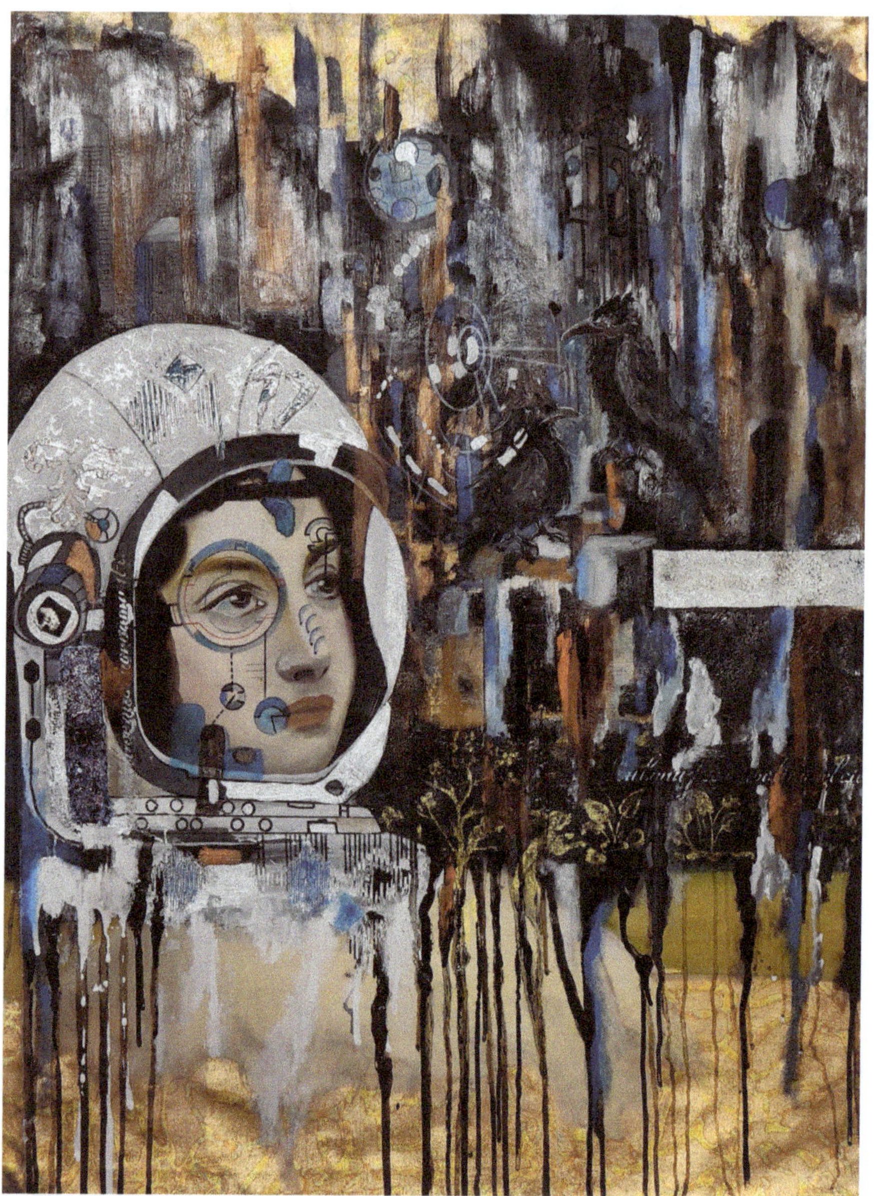

The Cartography of Seeing

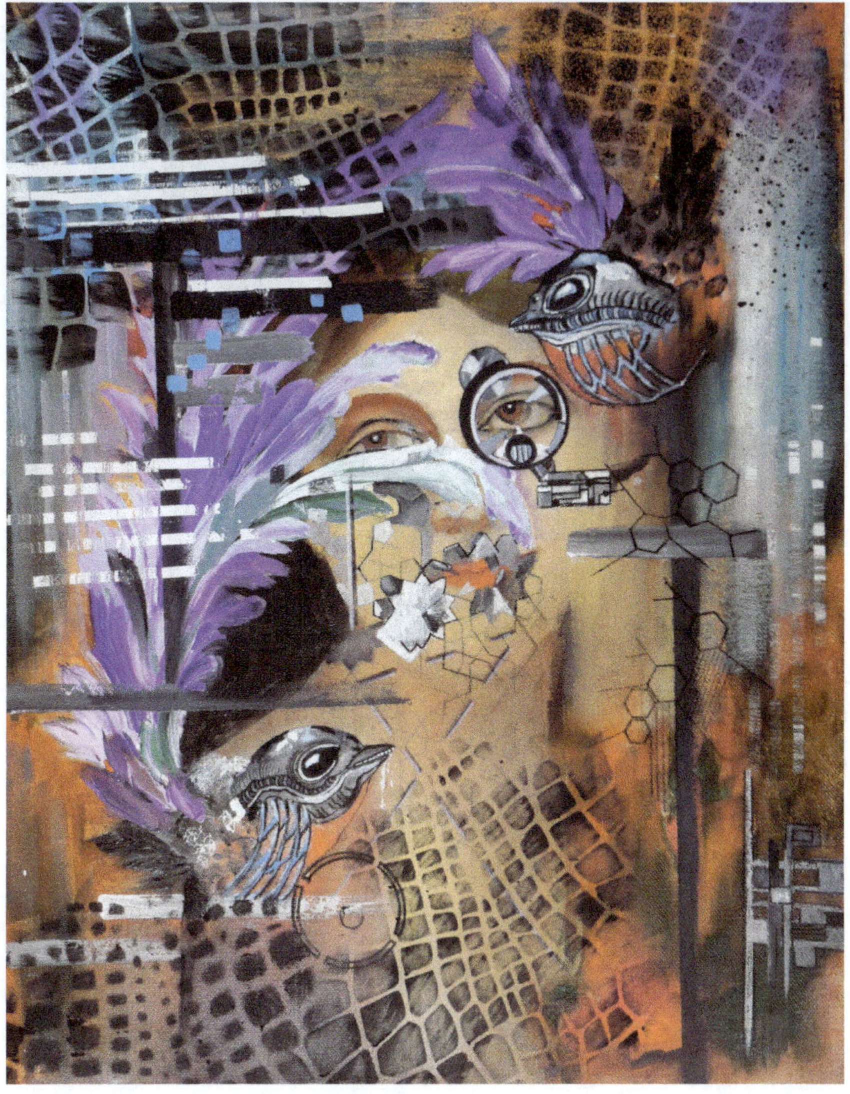

Transmissions from the Self

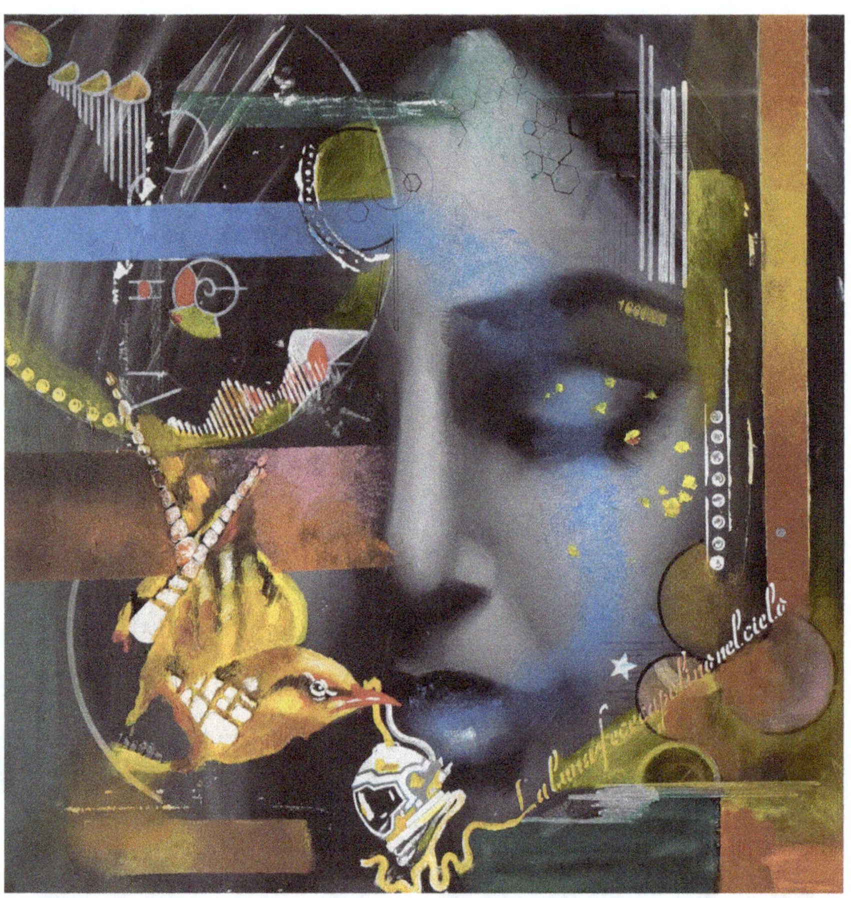

BRIAN KOMEI DEMPSTER

Planet

Across horizons, I don't know where it ends—floods
                        in houses, smoke from forests, bomb shrouds

     over Ukraine, ripped
                Gaza strip, borders torn, this war

        between violet and orange, Brendan clenching

           the crayon, his scribbles a tangled, cosmic
ball, tumbleweed careening

             across the page. Our bruised, burning
     world. My son, 20, these shapes part

         his own, part my hand

that guides him—*What do you see?*
              I grasp his wrist, the wax tip

         skitters, he blazes
    red trails, and I wonder

            if he's painting our yard, the maple's bright

scatter, remembering sky's apocalypse, ash-filled
           windows, the days Paradise

              burned, we shut ourselves
        inside, because he wouldn't wear

the mask, kept ripping it off his face, *Stop*

             Brendan, the smoke is toxic. He snatches up
    silver, dashes a frantic blizzard, and I wonder

if he senses bullets, understands
words like *school drill, active shooter,*

why his aide holds him still

beneath his desk
while he trembles, makeshift altars

and their jars of flowers. I am following
him into his world, these shadow

faces, half-moon craters, sadness

in the slow sweep
of his hand, rain he sprinkles

across the field. I am walking with him
across this planet, looking

for a blank stretch of calm

where we can hover, I can hand him
the gold. *Hai hai* my son hums

as he grasps
it, gilds the hollows, filling in light

helps me bandage shores

over a sea of bleeding
green, curve lines into wings, a bird lifting

from the whirlwind—flight dashed
above craters

and spills, shrapnel and teeming

foam. Maybe this
is a map, and he is telling us—

we might make it there, find

                                a place to land, his hand

       shaping the way.

WYN COOPER

No Two Alike

Rain rained down
through the space between us,
landed on our upturned hands.

Days ticked by, the half-full cup
now empty as the nest
the phoebes built last spring
on our back porch, nest
the tentworms overtook
until we torched it, flames
that almost lit the house on fire.

Ashes drifted down a minute later
from the high pine rafters
that held the roof that kept
us dry together up.

Down we went, ashes in still air,
or snowflakes, no two alike
they say but who are they
who cannot know how cold it was
in that long minute.

RACHEL HADAS

Bad Animal

All morning rumbling trucks hauled load on load
of gravel to repair a washed-out road.
One year ago we had torrential rain;
this year- precisely the same date – again.
This week two Joe's Brook farmhands had to go
home to Jamaica to repair their own
houses there, battered by the same huge storm
on its path northward.
       Now, in gentle weather,
the drying grass soft green, the day's heat done,
four friends growing old together
have met for dinner outside on the lawn,
beets and cucumbers from the flooded farm.
"We're a bad animal," someone says,
and no one disagrees. Bad animal:
so clever, so ingenious, so quick
to improvise repairs after the fact,
so slow to own the damage we have done,
and slower to agree,
to weigh the right next act, what we should do,
and do not only with a load of gravel.
How to unravel
the mess we've made, how to root out the old
tangle of instinct slimier than mold,
to extricate some hopeful, makeshift good
from each recurring and disastrous flood?
That evening, tranquil moon. The next day, sun.
And then it rained again.

RACHEL HADAS

A Walk Down Reeve's Driveway

Last day of hunting season.
Nothing was out: no hunter and no prey.
Nine o'clock. In the tick and hiss of snow
starting to fall, I walked the mile
to where the driveway ended and the road
began, and stopped, and stood.

Venus the night before
had hung on the horizon, huge and gleaming.
But what I now looked up to was a mild
blur behind branches. Whitening underfoot,
the road rhymed with the pallor of a sky
scarcely dark, as though it were still day.

EILEEN CLEARY

Spirit, Leave Me

If you won't speak, stop ruining my sleep.

We doze to cool off red cruelties of the day.
The burns beneath our skin: don't you remember

them? Oh. You've been crying again. Here, I've picked hyacinths.
Visit as long as you need. Listen, I can no longer rue I didn't leave
with you.

My grandchild was born. I had a talk with your make-believe
daughter Elizabeth, named before your menarche & never
swaddled before your

scarlet dried. Who's to say who exists? She forgives you for being
afraid to birth her. She'll explain that I am engineered to love this
new one

past the waters of Lethe. I am so often
at your deathbed. The terrible gathering
where some who never cherished you circled.

You could no longer carry them, so they hauled off
your books, scrawled *mine* on your things &
after the divvying, traded you for tickets. Were you

lighter then? They never saw the movie, you
forty years ago, a girl hammering wild heels
against your bedroom door, you floating through

the living room, amazed it didn't hurt
anymore to swim. *Shhh. Shhhh.*
I will send Elizabeth in case you need anything.

EILEEN CLEARY

Abecedarian: Red's Trial Preparation, Special Victims Room, Five Months Post Discharge from the Pediatric ICU

Accompanied by her nurse. the girl
barely audible, whispers, "Hi."

Can you tell me your name? If you ever
don't know the answer, just say so, Okay?
Every toy in this room is okay to use. Is that your
favorite stuffed animal? "Mama
gave me this bear." *Do you know why we're*
here today? Red fingers the rope-like scar on her neck.
"I got hurt."   *Do you remember that day?*

"Just a little bit."   *You aren't in trouble.*   "I
know I am." *I said aren't. Sweetheart, you are not.* Red
looks to her shoes. *What happened wasn't your fault.*   "Where's
Mama?"   *You'll see her soon. Wolf will be his own lawyer in court. He will ask:*

Nobody else saw you in the woods that day, right?
Only you know you were alone? In the cabin, did you try
pushing away? Did you say no? *And harder*
questions,   You petted me at first? Liked my fur? Asked me to follow? Why didn't you
run? Did you stay because you wanted me? Did you
scream or just lie there?   "I couldn't, my voice was stuck in my neck."

Try your best to answer yes or no.
Unless you'd like to, don't look at him. Your
victim advocate can sit next to you in court. Oh and Wolf will ask:

What were you wearing? Weren't your snacks there to lure me?
Explain what you were doing in the forest. Didn't
you trespass on my property?
Zigzagging through the woods like that, what did you expect?

EILEEN CLEARY

Why Red Doesn't Speak

Because a virgin was offered to a wolf.
Because fire's given to men in packs.
Because the cape was itchy and the sky damp wool.
Because nobody asked.
Because even an up close star becomes ambiguous.
Because they keep saying mother filled that wicker with cake and wine.
Because her mother drank paregoric and forgot to pack the basket.
Because of agonal respirations. Mother. Sweating. *Go to your grandmother.*
Because Red filled cardboard with canned tuna and the bread heels rummaged
    from the trash.
Because the cabin's air was skunk cabbage.
Because lilacs, or a willow, or honeysuckle summoned her outside.
Because he follows her—matted, ugly. Funky odor of wet fur in a frame of trees.
Because she still recalls the blue scent of cornflower and Edelweiss.
Because she was never safe or undressed at the same time.
Because wolves in men's clothing do not allow both in the woods.
Because woods are everywhere.

ESTHER LIN

The Wilderness

Clearing a way through wilderness is
the glassmaker's first task. She works far from
townfolk—she must—for the timbers with which
she melts soda, silica, and lime upon

her iron wand, from which she unrolls limpid
glass. The glassmaker is a witch—from flecks
of gold, tin, and cobalt, colors arise.
Unlike the glazier, who cuts and joins shapes

of sons and fathers, she devises pure
geometries. The glassmaker is the
devil. Black are the creases of her palms,

which raise the wand. Black are her lips, which puff
a perfect red sphere. A little planet
of air, earth, fire, and the blood in her veins.

ESTHER LIN

I Welcomed Its Spirit

Slain in the spirit, revived by the lord! This
one duty of Pentecostals like me.
There are others. One summer the minister
drove me and eight more children from New York

to Florida. We slept on linoleum,
sang hymns to boarded houses, handed out
cold water and cans of meat. Sometimes men
chased us with fists. We felt like martyrs. A boy

I liked thanked me for my Christ-like service.
Such a puny reward. Indeed, my faith
was humiliated to be so honored.

I learned how to hate. I welcomed its
spirit. I called for blood to rise in the fields.
I called a crusade against my enemy.

MICHAEL TYRELL

Cain's Disappointment

[He says]
In your childhood I tried stadiums, waves made of people, mascots like heroes
minus the weight of backstory–but you only wanted Story, especially wherever it
broke, people not obeying the laws of civility,
let alone the love of a game.

You who lived in those gaps.
You who if there were a Tree of Secrets, that would be what you would eat from.
Wandering, I didn't kill you so much as give you another story.

And look where it's gotten you–another brotherless summer, the limit of a jetty
where you stand wondering if I'm located there, in a borough across a river, or in
the belly of the river.

Is it all metaphor to people like you–you who turn a ward number into paradise?

Do you think I mind that you don't answer?

Can't you see I'm dissolving?

[And I say] I love you, brother, like something in both worlds.

Like the wet stilts of the jetty shining like the legs of racehorses, in salt.

MICHAEL TYRELL

Home

The good news: a new home's been found many light years away. Everyone has to hurry, the starships won't wait. A girl who's all packed goes to her house to collect her father, who like an intractable child has packed nothing. Hurry, this isn't funny, she says. He shakes his head. We're missing it, she cries. You can go on, he tells her, but I'm staying. Always someone you can't even go to the stars without. An alarm she hears going off—a light she sees, hurry, then earth without light. Let them go, he says, they're taking it with them, not the light, not the earth, but the dirt, the ruin…

I read this story once and can't find it now. Now that I need it, I can't find it. It's not the end of the world, I tell the jonquils, even though the fact you're here in January probably means it is the end of the world. The flowers are DIY'ing a night sky, bashful and yellow on the ground. It doesn't matter there's nobody here yet to tell me to hurry. I'm still the one who wants to remain and disappear at once. The evenings turn warmer. The shop windows fill with suitcases.

MICHAEL TYRELL

Café Vertigo

In the movie, when the revenant appears,
every detail has to be perfect
for the spell to work; she must
wear the hairstyle and suit
the hero saw her die in,
when he thought he saw her fall–

And it doesn't matter he's wrong
about the whole thing; she never
died to begin with; it's only his misunderstanding
and the green light through the hotel room window
that approximate resurrection.

Walking hours after dark—
you're doing what the hero does in the movie,
the same loop of leaving and arrival–

As tonight, recognizing the CAFÉ sign from some earlier era
floating two stories above the bar whose name
said aloud sounds like the word keys–
the sign that same green as the resurrection
scene in the movie–

Is every survivor an imposter?
Why call anything so temporary *home*?
Shouldn't it be funeral *hotel*, not home?
You wander inside like a hotel guest
under a light algae and unreliable
as sun through pond ice,
seeking the ones who won't let you
stay dead or change into someone else.
Who's been dressing you up every day
in the threads of the past?

JENNIFER MILITELLO

Wax Self-Portrait /

[sometimes there is a story still inside like a fish caught and flayed and eaten for its flesh]

[there is a protocol for living by sins whispered in the confessional to a man who is not the priest]

[there is a protocol for pathways choked by memory or a desire or pressure at the back of the neck]

[there is a protocol for terror, for the throat closing up]

[there is a protocol for being fed at the wolf's mouth, at the mother's breast]

[for bringing trash cans out and back]

[there is a protocol, listen: momentum falling like a noose]

[stimuli hooved in their tracks, agnostic as beasts]

[no one crouches down among wild raspberries just to be scratched by thorns]

[there is no such indeed as breathing, there is no such indeed as faith]

JENNIFER MILITELLO

The Ten Commandments of the Anatomist's Wife /

Thou shalt not let the tissue sample go toxic.

Thou shalt not let the scalpel scrape.

Honor the theater of the operation,

the breeding of deathbeds in its depths.

Thou shalt not covet thy neighbor's eye or tibia

or the godless handle that is his heart.

Thou shalt not let injury fingerprint the herd.

Halt thy vast intelligences in the ways they reach.

Halt the origins, their burnt and wild hymns.

Remember the solemn jugs insomnia tips.

The body is a god. Worship no other.

Thou shalt not take the body's name in vain.

PATRICK DONNELLY

Prayer without a God

> —substituting a colon where the word "Lord" might have
> appeared during my Age of Faith, but when I speak it, I
> still have to say the word

I'm so small :

minuscule as a doll's roller skate

found in the lawn, mistaken

at first for a molar.

Weak : as a battery smelling of sulfur,

exhausted with all

the ascending, traversing, and descending

it's had to power.

One finds structures of terrifying beauty

in the visions from space telescopes. Pillars of plasma,

neon, filaments, dusty sheaths gushing lightning,

gushing potentialities.

It may rain diamonds on Neptune.

On this planet, it rains rain.

On this planet, some pray for justice to swing low,

touch down like rain.

From this planet, if I could look through a lens,
I might spy the vast longing of my unimportance,

lonesome mote floating
across infinity's ruthless eyeball.

: : : : : : : : : Once
in occupied Paris,

an SS officer beckoned to a boy
who had his sweater inside out

to hide the yellow star.
Out after curfew,

he expected the worst.
Maybe it was raining,

God willing; it was within the bounds
of possibility that rain

was trying to wash Europe
clean.

But the Nazi picked him up,
hugged him,

showed him from his wallet a yellowed photo
of a little boy.

Gave him some money.
Beckon, hug, photo, money.

Does the *order* matter? Though it's as mere
as one dot of ink

riding atop
another dot of ink.

Twin singularities,
swallowing worldly effects.

Goethe's absent
umlaut.

An Inquisitor's
vampire bite

on Galileo's
starful throat.

PATRICK DONNELLY

Notes on Necromancy

33. The lilies withered
then stank. Song
of descents.

32. Yes, you lost someone, then ached
until your sex baked dry.

31. But why raise with dark arts
poor Michael of the blue
five o'clock shadow,

30. if only back to his sick room
with its tulips and tissues?

29. If he's moved on.
Hasn't he moved on?

28. To limitless light, the heaven of the Moon?

27. Whether it's an abomination
to empty a grave depends
on who, why, and depth of imagination.

26. Warning:

25. Do it, and you'll pay a price.

24. Very dear.

23. You might weep deep
trenches of black hyssop down
your presuming cheeks.

22. For using craft against nature
and the stupid, stupid horse

that dying rode in on.

21. The *materia* are filthy:
burnt mullein, grave dirt,
pentacles of wax, a monkey's paw.

20. Alhough, it's said Gangshar Wangpo
was revived from death
by a breeze Trungpa Rinpoche
caused when he moved:

19. Some spread life
where'er they walk.

18. Jesus, his disciples, Elijah, Elisha, etc.
Raising, being raised, raising oneself—

17. Scheherazade told stories
to stay alive.

16. But what story
if one wishes
to stay dead?

15. Rilke, while sympathetic,
roasted Orpheus
for loving Eurydice
back to their life.

14. After she had moved on
inside herself, no longer any man's.

13. Cool gales shall fan the glade.

12. Don't head down the long ramp
with a lyre, a fucking lyre.

11. Don't make a big
opera about everything.

10. You could try allowing yourself
to be consoled for once.

9. Trees, where you sit, shall crowd into a shade:

8. Michael Haley

7. Ken Ketwig

6. Robbie Mittle

5. Ramon Castaneda

4. Terry Cook...

3. Bewildering:

2. On the front, the Emerald Tablet says: Don't.

1. But the back still says: You could.

Turn Point

1. What
yanks
the spine-
studded rock-
fish with its five-
star Michelin hook
reels me up too & too fast
past the languid opium-
ribboned furls of jade sea
kelp forests rushing us
past the incessant sway
-ing of blue ocean skin
where some say ebb first
merges with flood in a
single molecule of
water which is what
some claim pulls us
past the old Turn

2.
up
a-
of
to
&
an
of
ni-
I

3. Point lighthouse
on the jagged cliff
shore what pulls us out
enrapt devotion
plunging blackness
what abruptly breaks
invisible seal
aquatic equa-
-mity & now
must catch
my breath as we await
the scalpel slicing
our shared nerve fibers
to run its course.
4. There is not in any world
any adequate word to
express no good
way to say how
we relate or how
we resonate with
nothingness as if
beyond our senses it's
always present so we eye
each other's eyes round
5. tires with nothing – round

6.
not
spare.
Unlike
him I'll
sprout two
spindly legs
and step away
from the wood
planks bruising
our wet shingled
scales. Battered: I

7. avoid the skillet
but in exchange for human
lungs something must be given
up that my faithful friend cannot
himself surrender. I do not know how
I could stand to watch his flailing grow-
ing ever-slower how I could stand to watch his
shape setting solid while his wide button solar-
eclipse eyes watched me flop beside. Both our fits
grew slower but as our serrated spines disconnected
there I stood alone pulling room air   fluently. Under
hushed hours littered by rest-notes looming to become
their inverse to say some silent line of confluence
has split so he must be he and I must be me and
his fixed image will soon turn into a story I'll
tell my lover in another existence I can't yet
place. With my nimble legs I'll slip between
a bent length of barbed wire fence tracing
the veiled tract of land behind the light-
house keeper's cabin where my love - the
keeper's cook - sleeps his face serene his dream-
tides receding into a raw uncut marble backdrop.
Before curation before Michelangelo thought to
think to angle his chisels his vision before his
massive stone muse had left the old quarries of
Carrara bound off for Firenze by heft by hoof by
boat yet to dazzle yet to freeze or please or take
the form of man when David was naked mount-
ain he was complete by way of what he was
without. When I see my love asleep I see
mountain. When I see my love awake – –
still mountain. What makes it so magni-
ficent is ranging his earthen scape
with saltwater still pooling at my
feet as cold air seeps through
thin cracks quietly defining
those dim sapphire-edged
window sills like eyes
locked together like eye-
lids fluttering when the ever-
darkening flank between us is just
jagged crusted sea salt dripping dusk
what hooks his lips to mine. Abrupt.

1

ERICA GOODKIND

Read All About It
Abecedarian, for Bob Ross

all the news that's fit to
break your heart, to fill your fragile empty
cup with rushing venom, an ooze of blood, an oil spill, then
drain it fast, so that, left in a craving state, you want more. What
elegant devils we serve, we drink for breakfast. Misery's one helluva
franchise: recession-proof, monopolizer of moods, and the audacity to
go door-to-door   with its shark-skin suitcase selling weak dopamine
hits on the side.   An abusive relationship, like any prudent parasite,
insists on not killing its host. Beguiled by the night, one eye turns blind as
jackals yip alongside, burying heads in plain sight. An ostrich almost
killed Johnny Cash once out walking the hills. Its claw-toed Bruce
Lee stop-kick flicked like a snake tongue, landed smack in the
middle of the Man-in-Black's belt buckle. Trusty old iron.
Neither had been looking for trouble and neither had
put his eyes in the sand at the reality clash. At San
Quentin the musician put sun in dark spaces –
ruffling her beak into shallow soft ground
several times a day an ostrich gently
turns her incubating eggs around,
unaware that people think her
virtue to nurture is a silly
weakness. Wrists flick
Xtra, xtra! calling slick
yoyos back to hands, to
zip down, zip up again.

I Am Not a Man-Hater, Just Quasi-Buddhist

Have dinner ready.
Plan ahead, even the night before, to have a delicious meal ready on time. This is a way of letting him know that you have been thinking about him and are concerned about his needs. Most men are hungry when they come home and the prospect of a good meal is part of the warm welcome needed.

Prepare yourself.
Take fifteen minutes to rest so that you are refreshed when he arrives. Touch up your makeup, put a ribbon in your hair and be fresh looking. He has just been with a lot of work-weary people. Be a little gay and a little more interesting. His boring day may need a lift.

Clear away the clutter.
Make one last trip through the main part of the house. Gather up the books, toys, and newspapers. Dust the tables so that they appear clean. Your husband will feel that he has reached his haven of rest and order. Doing this for him will give you a lift also.

Prepare the children.
Take a few minutes to wash their faces and hands. Comb their hair and change their clothes if it is necessary to make them look presentable to him. They are God's "Creatures" and your husband would like to see them playing their part.

Minimize all noise.
At the time of his arrival, eliminate all the noises of the washer, dryer, dishwasher, and vacuum. You've had plenty of time to do these things during the day. Don't do them now. Encourage your children to be quiet. Be happy to see your husband. Greet him with a warm smile.

Do not greet your husband with problems or complaints.
Don't complain when he is late for dinner. Count this as minor when compared to what he had to go through today.

Make him comfortable.
Have him lean back in a comfortable chair or suggest that he lie down for a few minutes in the bedroom. Have a cool or warm drink ready for him. Arrange his pillow and offer to take off his shoes. Speak in a low, soft, soothing and pleasant voice. Allow him to relax and unwind.

Listen to him.
You may have a dozen things to tell him but the moment of his arrival is not the time. Let him speak first.

Make the evening his.
He is special! Never complain that he does not take you out to dinner or to other pleasant entertainment. Instead, try to understand his world of strain and pressure, his need to unwind and relax. Remember that you relaxed all day waiting for his return. Now it's his turn to enjoy what you enjoyed. **Try to make his home a place of peace and order, a place where your husband can relax in body and spirit.**

Erasure Elegy for the National Endowment for the Arts

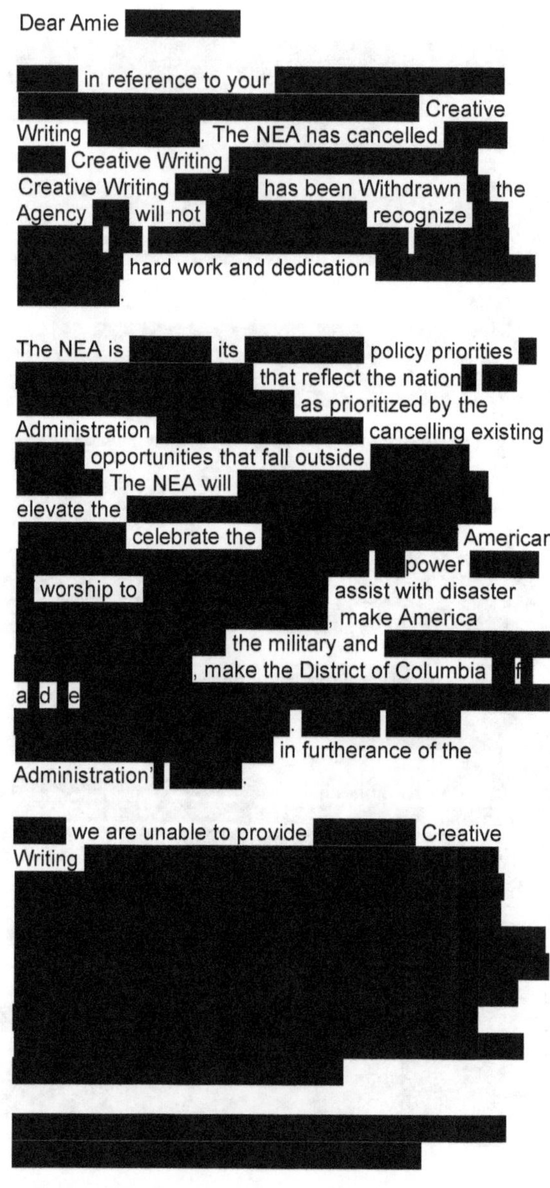

Sincerely,
The National Endowment for the Arts

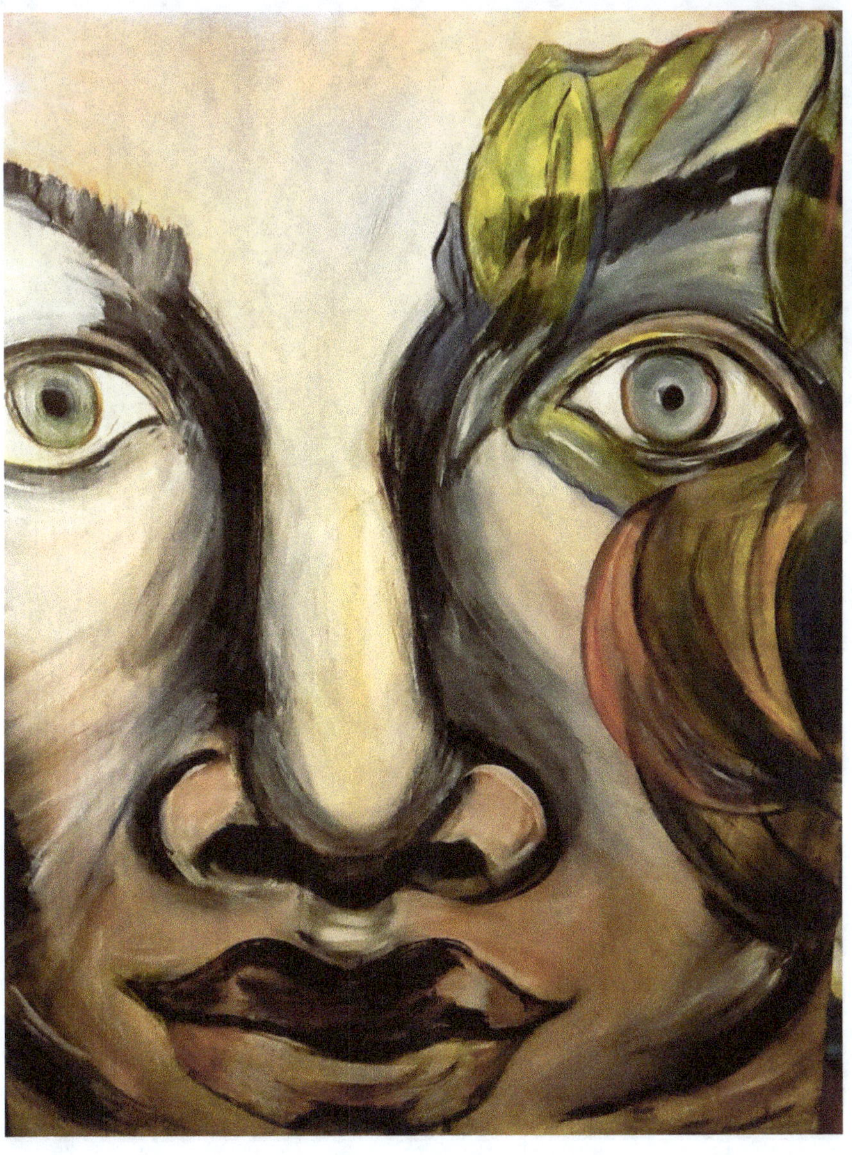

Life Underwater

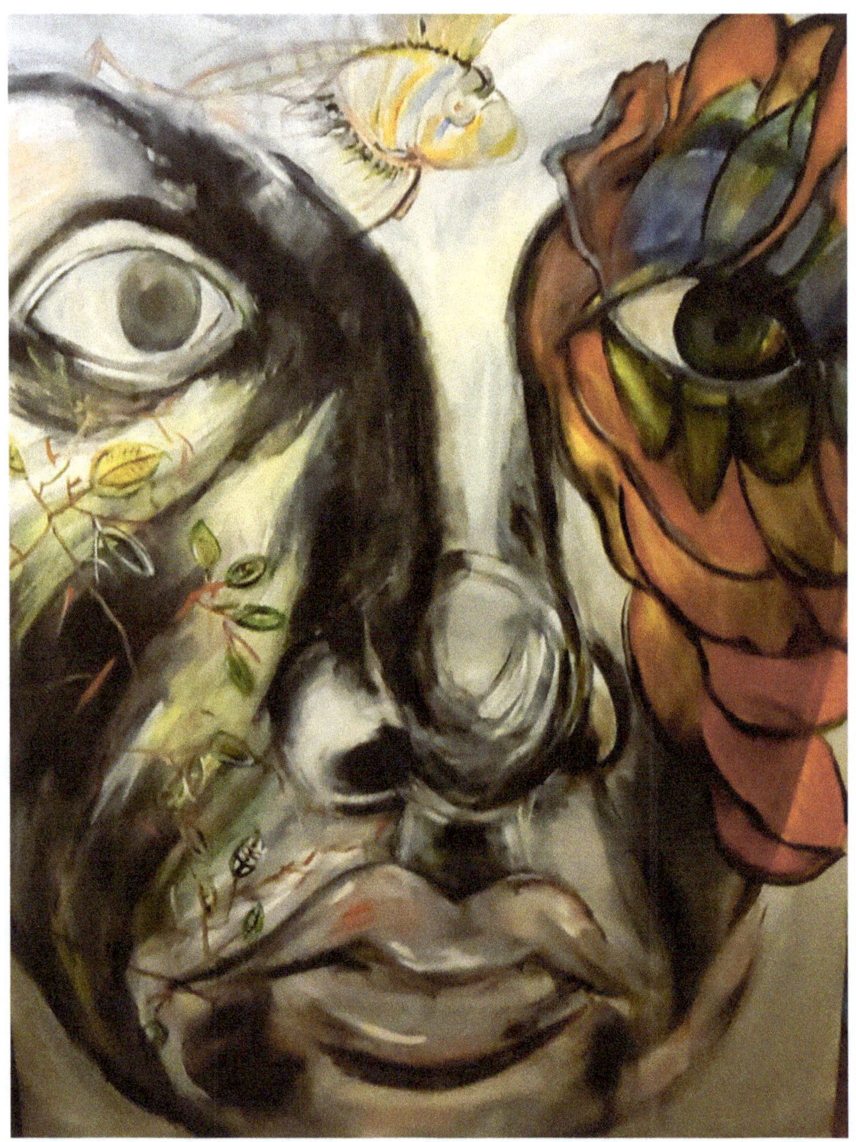

Primavera

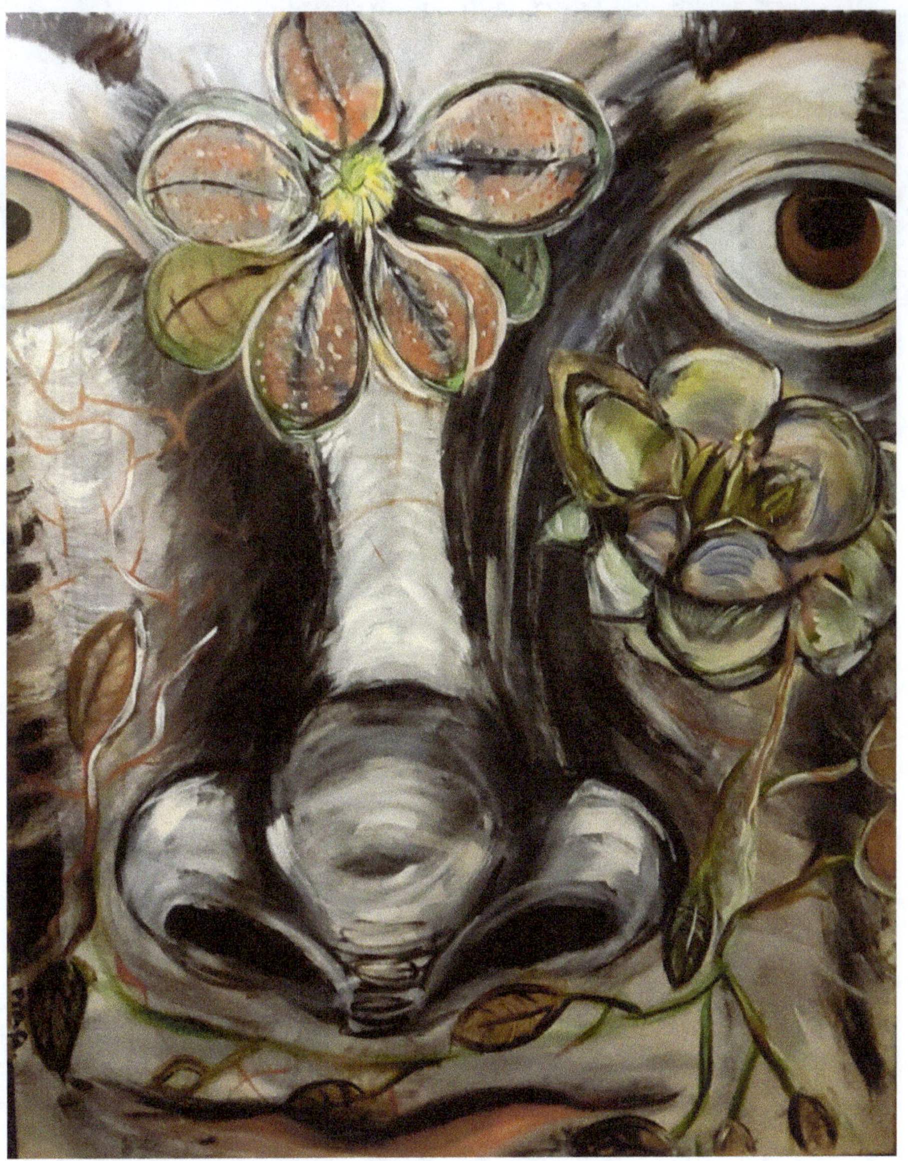

KATIE FARRIS

St. Finbarr's South, Cork, Ireland

I slipped 20E in the old oak box and lit ten candles
in their ruby red jars with the USB-C rechargeable
lighter. The candles were only 30p, but my
fourth great-grandmother emigrated around 1851
and I thought we owed some back tithes. St. Finbarr
means St. Tow Head, reminding me of my little
brunette brother's infant white-blonde ringlets,

his face a grubby telegram of one thrifty word:
lost. In the little parish bathroom, a
cracked bar of soap and an old looped cloth towel
dispenser. The church was engaged in missions
of poverty, built as it was in the age of Catholic
death: tenements, rotted potatoes, and my mother's
mother's mother's mother's mother's

mother in the heart of it, in Skibbereen,
starving but not dying so that my mother, in West Virginia,
could suck on rhubarb from her mother's garden
when she was hungry. All I had left in my
pockets was a dime, but I left that too,
behind. I slipped out, a cryptid in the dusk. A survivor,
returned. A ghost amidst the Virgin's roses.

KATIE FARRIS

The Metamorphosis Along the Seine

Along the Seine, not far from Notre Dame,
a man comes under the bridge, alights
bird-like on the metal railing along the
water, dips his hand like a bird's beak

into the river, comes up dripping and
drapes the water along his bald pate
like a silk scarf. Again, the beak and again,
he spreads the Seine along his face.

Removes his shoes. Looking up, the
old fluorescent tube lights so luxuriously
swathed in cobwebbed dust they blend
against the limestone, smoked antique,

this bridge stamped N for Napoleon,
made of limestone which, made wet,
gets whiter with time. He claps. Measures
the sound against his ears, moves a few

meters, claps again. The water surges as
the curve under the bridge captures
the sound, bounces it back. Satisfied
this second time, he bobs, splashes away. His

shoes, left behind, loll open on the quai.

CHRISTOPHER BAKKEN

Morning Sea

Don't make me stop. Don't make me see
the way a small fishing boat, even when
stalled on blocks for winter, reflects sun
from its dingy hull, on a morning
too bright to be trusted.

Don't make me stand. Let me deny what I see
(I didn't look long—the boat might not be real).
Let me drag my gaze from where it caught,
and run, not looking back, never
insulting what's still here.

CHRISTOPHER BAKKEN

January Swim

First dive of the year, lured into the cove
    by the old stone dragons of Ierissos,
who have, by January, converted the water to flame

—thinking of my friend Adam, who would float
    for hours at Chora Sfakion on Crete,
or, other summers, at the placid edge of Kos or Kardamyli.

He once wrote from Preveli, impressed
     by the *wild, muscular orthodoxy*
conveyed by the statue of a monk with a machine gun.

He sometimes settled for Sardinia,
    though he would have loved Ierissos, had he
not died last April in Krakow. He last wrote at Easter,

said he was busy scribbling poems and shaping
    something on Brodsky—that my new son
had arrived with a message: *The future exists. Don't worry.*

He loved lindens and Gregorian chant
    (in small doses, taken like a potion).
He was a poet of doubt and rapture,

always moored to earth by books, black cats,
    and the sight of his beloved wife's face.
Swimming too. And Seferis' great poem, "The King of Asini,"

inspired by a Homeric footnote.
    At Ierissos, my wife and son are pacing the sand.
We have a long drive to reach the future. I am shivering,

and very tired of death (*just sadness, that's all*),
     like Seferis in 1945,
wrung out by war, and distrustful of words, but suddenly moved

when a blind man in Athens made his way
     past the bullet-riddled walls and stepped right
into the fire, playing Greek anthems on his harmonica.

Adam was born that same year in Lvov,
     to a Europe of shabby anthems, sublime
blindness—with all the wounds Seferis promised. Also, the sea

CHRISTOPHER BAKKEN

A Defense of Poetry

A harbor town empty this afternoon
of all consolation by the time
the martyred letters had been erased.
No reflections hurry past
the papered glass of the shop window.
The heat's blare is muted by no breeze.
No time for oracles now:
not even a radio will sing this late.
Blank gaze of linen pinned to a line.
A mocking ceremony of geranium.
The stupidity of mortar and stone
against the perfect sea's monotony.
Yet there, at the end of the dock, someone
taut with concentration, almost
immobile—a statue, maybe—is hauling
fist over fist an invisible net, heavy
as the air soars through it, ignites
the gills of fish gasping in their pail.

STEPH KLEID

The Truest Thing I Know

is that I know nothing
except—this:

someday someone I love will leave
what's left of me to brine in the Atlantic
alongside the leatherback sea turtles
of which I know nothing except—
adoration and someday all my ink will pale
or burn or find someone who knows nothing
of what it meant to have been right
here right now except—I was frantic
and here and wild and rambling and round
and hungry and here and naked and warm
and here and heavy and here and calling
and they will know nothing except—

I was

                here

     I was

                      I was

JUSTIN WYMER

When I Was a Body, I Was a Boy

In my first brush with pleasure with another, you
walked in. Simple as that. The queen stood threadbare
in the smoke-damp, squat room at the back of the hall
wide enough for two boys to risk, tense-jawed, their lives
for an instant of being, beheld by warmth not fixed
to tealights on the wall, illumining Jesus' side—chiseled, rent
with arrows, eyes eager. His wounds corresponded
to ones we'd given ourselves, as we longed for his lithe hew
to round us up, brethren, and embrace us nice. Then
you walked in. It was your room, after all. Your gold
doorknob with its one slit for shiv-like key twisted
and I saw you seeing what you'd always surmised:

I won't give you this, Mother. That's what I should've said.
Not jolted like a tick, burnt dead in your bed.

JUSTIN WYMER

My Mother's Garden

Sunflower, eye-prismed, can you find home?
My mother bolts red, in roots green in your shade.

Lamb's ear, is your velvet a gift or defense?
My mother is safe, locked as sugar in sap.

Morning, who lit the tower in your cloud on fire?
My mother leapt out her window into a carnation.

Cricket, so delicate, do you cry from ash in your throat?
My mother is an archive up in flame.

Pond-frog, flint-voiced, why nag me, *Think of legacy?*
Gnats swarm the holes in my mother's name.

Fountain, pool of nothing, does the dove dive in to heal?
My mother blooms through my hand like blood in lace.

Red cloth, why are you here, among the healthy tulips?
My mother wore a blindfold to block out choices.

Peony, swaying with ants, are you mother or prisoner?
My mother stopped trying to step out the door.

Crabapple windfall, must you molder in that dress?
I'll leave, past the gate. For my mother I'll be some happiness.

CARIDAD MORO-GRONLIER

Did You Ever Learn How to Dance?

At parties I sat tabled and watched
the other fathers waltz their daughters
across the floor. Their girls demure
as the dapper daddies smiled
down on them. I waited for Papi
to extend his hand and lead us out
toward the center of the room,
but even though he tapped his toes
to every tune, he never looked my way.

At home I begged the mirror to explain.
I blamed my freckles, my braces,
the image of my mother
stamped on my face, reminder
of the wife who left. So much
time I spent hating myself,
I never thought to ask.

JESSICA CUELLO

Feral Mouths to Feed

I was no one's favorite, no one's anticipation,
and the soft creature we longed for arrived
out of the blue. It was our fifth apartment,
the first to allow a cat, and we named her
Nancy because we never got close enough
to see that she was a boy. The day she leapt
on the counter and stole the bacon, we rooted
for her, for her bold hunger as our father ran
after her across the yard, over the invisible
line to the landlord side. They fought a tug-
of-war and he yanked the bacon free, triumphant,
Nancy's little body briefly suspended in air.
Soon after the battle Nancy fled the same way
she arrived: unwanted and free, and for years
my brother spoke mournfully of Nancy as if
she had belonged to him, as if she was the only
cat he'd ever loved though they had never touched,
her attention meager, even though other cats came
later, and their saucers of store-bought, wet food
meant a wild bounty Nancy would never know.

JESSICA CUELLO

Jane Eyre's Love

Whose face did I have after all?
Little Adèle had her mother's

careless eye, her loose way.
Coquetry in her blood said

Mr. Rochester. *It's not her fault*
said Jane, who taught Adèle

as though she were loved, and
one time in first grade I arrived

without shoes, just the heavy
snow boots, ugly boy boots,

clunking on the classroom rug.
I cried so hard from shame

the teacher called my father up.
He came, my pair of sneakers

in hand. He'd been my father
a whole year. But the time after,

when I threw up, no one came
and the school sent me to my aunt's

where I tugged and tugged
at the screen door. I knew

my face kept me locked out.
There was a man inside it,

looking out my eyes and turning
down my mouth. When I gave up

on the latch, and sat, severed,
from the house, from myself,

for years, I heard Jane call out
from inside the red room, saw

her arms touch the neck
of little Helen Burns—

and I touched my own cheek
with the soft paper seam.

KATE MACLAUCHLAN

Ghazal for Icarus's Wings

Call me culprit, cause of demise, though the fault was not mine.
Flawless design, feathered object of blame for a climb not mine.

Diligent father, fulfilling the promise to protect, to keep his son alive.
But the gap between *alive* & *living*– his misunderstanding, not mine.

What of the son, who sensed a history dissociated from bloodline,
not yet able to speak what he sought? His divergence, not mine.

I carried the weight of their missed attempts, not from absence
of love, but from mouths inert as sound in an underground mine.

Easier to condemn me as cause and effect, than to admit no one is
culpable. Icarus, Daedalus, altitudes of their own making, not mine.

KATE MACLAUCHLAN

Rosemary

My grandmother, in hospice and drunk on morphine,
        kept lifting her hand to the sky, repeating the word
Rosemary. Doctors thought that she, a devout Catholic,

was requesting a rosary, rather than saying the name
        of her sister, who died of epilepsy.
I envy the faithful– how their chests, by falling prostrate,

lighten. My only experience of religion was a summer
        spent dancing, six days a week,
drilling repertory in a high school gymnasium. I attended

each muscle, like a rosary bead, chiseled it with devotion.
        Skin of my shoulder peeled away
by another girl's tights, rubbed raw and red by my belief

that if you repeat a movement countless times, push
        through exhaustion, the moment arrives
when your performance is flawless. I became a god fed

by evidence, secured my place in the heavens each time
        I lifted the girl on my shoulder.
How small I became, then, the day I touched down

on the tarmac and witnessed my grandmother mid-
        flawless moment, hand raised
to the sky, rounded by the sound of *Rosemary*.

KATE MACLAUCHLAN

To Venus Xtravaganza

*A transgender woman and performer associated with New York City's ball
culture scene. On December 21, 1988, Xtravaganza was found dead in
a room at the Fulton Hotel in New York City. Her body had been placed
under a mattress, and investigators determined she had been bound and
strangled. Angie Xtravaganza, her drag mother, was the first person
detectives contacted, and she later informed Venus's biological family.*

Behind you is a window. Beyond it: a world
that closes its hairy knuckles around the ruby neck
of a hummingbird. Still, you wear all white, swoop
your hair into a bun and proclaim: *I want to be
married in a church.* I press rewind, watch
those words roll, again, from your lips
with the same resolve as the ocean tide. You glide
down the runway, carry a golden handbag
with room enough to hold all of what you're owed.
Head resting on your hand, you confess you left
home because you *didn't want to embarrass them.*

When they find your body tucked under a mattress,
I imagine untangling your limbs, returning you
to that place where your light is the first to pierce the dark.

GRACE SCHULMAN

Gods in New York

Don't say the gods are dead. I see Minerva
in bronze, immense and owl-eyed, although
the journal she was cast to praise went under.
Walkers still set their watches by its bells.

The gods descend: Diana draws a bow
in risky balance on a slender foot.
Atlas holds heaven up. The trickster, Hermes,
slips in false train announcements at Grand Central.

I gaze at stone immortals at the Met.
Aphrodite lures as shiva dances.
Idols, too, are watchful, like the bull
that rears on traffic islands, warning drivers.

Once the prophet Habakkak barred worship
of wood or stone, now I, an unbeliever,
in an uncertain time, bow to the miracle
of bronze, zinc, copper, gold leaf, marble, stone.

GRACE SCHULMAN

Felled

White oaks down the block,
steeple-tall, knock-kneed,
for weeks endured

the whine of a chainsaw
clearing the land
for a new stucco house.

How they had stood
unshaken, carrying
sea-wind arpeggios

caught in their branches,
and voices that roared
in meaningless phrases.

sheltering toads
and common insects,
inviting horned lizards

to hide in their trunks,
and altar-white egrets
to curl in green leaves.

Now their cut logs
are piled on trucks
to reveal rings of history,

how workers dug ditches
in land once a swamp
now a fertile field,

how oaks shaded farmers,
smiths and bay fishers
from whitehot sun.

Now the absence between
two of the fallen
thrills with urgency

like the space between words.
Let them be there, in hiding,
like the road's shadows

invisible at sundown.
Let the last oak stand hardy
until it is struck

like the heart.

GRACE SCHULMAN

Going Back to Rapallo

1

The girl in this photo must be me,
caught in a snap while racing to the harbor.
Who was she really? Lankier than I,

wearing a sailor's straw hat and striped shirt,
hair blown to dance wild in the salt wind,
she breathes deep after leaping to clear

a landed skiff, feet bare (how could that be
on a beach stuck with stones?) voice rising
to a shout above the sea's commotion.

[Not shown here]: on the dock, a smiling man,
friend become first love become, she feared,
a house with locked doors; no way to find

the answers. She'll leave him in the autumn.

2

Who is she now, hair bound, come back at last
to the windswept beach, step, fermata, step,
no longer asking what she's searching for.

She knows the bright sea's undersides of griefs.
Now lulled by the litanies of waves
and by a sloop's sails, angel wings upwind,

she wants to tell the rangy straw-hat girl
how answers fade like breakers that spew froth
and then bow down, forgotten by the sea.

Same rocks here. Same umbrella pines
unfelled by the storm. All things are the same
except a woman whose speech flows under

the water's unremitting cadences.

AMY KING

Sit, Speak

It is the same woman, I know, for she is always creeping and most women do not creep by daylight. —Charlotte Perkins Gilman

Alone in a hearse,

Sugar bowl I sit

If memory works only backwards then why look ahead?

How can we know each other?

The Dad Walking Around In Your Head isn't even a ghost.
He's a mutilated version of man. A normal one. A rapist.

It's not as if you drink the sea alone.

Say it in lowercase for now.

We become the day before tomorrow but it's not the day before tomor-
row yet.

She who lives shall see

"Everyone sees noon at her doorstep."

It's the Call of the Void

Beckoning her back

Belly to background

Returning to sheep

A midday demon

Late is worth more than never.

The outfit won't make the monk or the nun.

The night brings advice in lieu.

A Ghost Eternity is really nothing more

than night sky unraveling forever.

The way your heart beats backward

Because you ghost the blood of one

You thought was you,

You bore boredom,

Your study in religion failed, you,

The one you thought never matters

The hurt heart stuff sent in ripped postscripts

in the hopes that someone hears and chooses.

You, a lost home seeking self,

the story we carry societally,

a society of altruists governed by psychopaths.

Inhale the rise of sound, lubed throat, guttural ink,

genius in your nostrils' scripted air.

If God is dead, then have we still to kill?

"How shall we comfort ourselves, murderers of all?"

You may fish for light

But must return to the sea

That to which it belongs.

The boat is made of boat

The dead child is a stone

You won't believe that the child in me died

I don't believe, me,

I believe in no one

Is it not fact if fantasy is the purveyor of what we believe

And how we breathe life into stones

Yet it is the only thing in the beginning to do:

The sea child is stone, returning to flight,

returning to fight.

DANA HENRY MARTIN

What I Call This Boy

I call him *boys will be boys*. I call him
the one who beats a man and leaves

him for dead without consequences.
The one who smashes a teenager's

car with a length of pipe while the kid's
in it, glass shattering all around him,

which lets in the boy's screaming
and laughter. The one in the shed

huffing gasoline who gets so high
he thinks he's floating away

from his father but he can never
do that because he's already

his father even though he's still
a boy. I call him the finger on

a throat, the hand on a rib, the knee
where knees shouldn't go, jolting

to the boy's tacit orders. I call him
a boy who gets what he wants,

one who explodes like fireworks
in a forgotten shoulder of a town.

I call him automatic. Boy body like
a weapon. Mouth shooting blanks.

Wear your armor around this one,
this boy who learned how to boy

from men who were once boys
and wish they could still be boys

so they boy the boys out of their own
boys in order to live through them

and still feel like boys. To boy again!
The panties. The cleavage. The taking.

The yanking. The tearing. The breaking.
The skinning. The slapping. The shaking.

The fucking. The killing. The maiming.
The raping. To boy, to buoy hatred

and hormones on a raft of upturned
consciousness in a lake full of poison-

swollen bottom feeders and water snakes
that are almost as venomous as the boys

themselves. *Boys will be boys*. Behind
the convenience store. In the alley.

Along the water's edge. In the park.
In the classroom. On the playground.

In their homes. In ours. In our cars.
On our paths. On our sidewalks.

In our neighborhoods. In the creeks
behind our houses. In our backyards.

In our pools. In our hot tubs. In our
bedrooms. On the floor. On the ground.

In the weeds. Back by the water. Now
in the water. Now in the currents that

carry their boyhood across the state,
across the whole country, all the way

out to sea, where it meets up with all
the other boyhoods. And the water

loses its translucence. And the fish die.
And the waterfowl die. And the plants,

you guessed it, die. Until one day a boy
comes along and grabs an oyster, pries

it open, lets it slide down his throat pearls
and all, and boys who will be boys are

reborn through him. More and more boys
who will be boys. So many pearlescent,

watery, naked boys who are already full
of themselves and ready to devour the world.

DANA HENRY MARTIN

Crossroads

Father moved time around like a sorting puzzle, those
with a missing tile for shifting. There's only one way to stop

shiftiness like his: ram truth into the empty slot. You knew that,
Mother. The shifting was all the women and girls being passed

around, a kaleidoscope of blinding movement, a bling of bodies.
Truth was not his way. *Truth is not your way, is it, Jack?*

My trinity was fear, shame, and guilt. Mother, you didn't need a book
to teach me that. *You either, Jack. Guilt with its gilded edges,*

*its brocade, the silky red nightgown you had mom put me in
before you carried me to your bed.* I was the child who was used,

passed around. That child was me, but it wasn't only me. I wasn't
alone. Rocks dropped into drink glasses, tumblers full of broken seas.

No, it's that lake we all loved, Mother, especially you. The iron
waters of Texoma saved you, saved me, until I hit puberty

and men came royalling in, speeding past on their waxed boats,
all leer, loll, and bobble. When will you, when will you, come

back to me, Mother? I believe you. Your light hair and light eyes
pressed up against the sky. The big Oklahoma sky of our childhoods.

I know about the gangrene and Thorazine. Neither was your fault,
Mother. He smoked out the worst in men, called it his lodge.

He pseudo-peyoted others into silence and vomiting bliss. The poison
didn't take in you, or in me. Your little hands on udders, Mother,

at the farm. Your little mouth wrapped around a candy cigarette
as you ride on the back fender of your brother's bicycle. Your older

brother. Your good brother. You gave me a brother like that, too.
I see him now, flitting in the summer sun, tall as a scarecrow

guarding barren fields. I see the best in him. He was never
not like you. He learned to view the world through Father.

Thank you, Mother, for that good boy, that man who's tried
to believe your way of seeing his whole life. Thank you

for telling me to write, Mother. Thank you for telling me
to do whatever I had to in order to survive, including surviving

you. It was hard to see you through Father, his grit and grimace.
My chest hurts, Mother, and not in the poetic way. In the shuffle,

I managed to get dad's heart, that filched heat pump, its clomped
and clumped machinery bleating in this bleeding world.

      I think I'm dying, Mother.

I see your white linen dress flagging in the warm distance.
I can almost reach you. Mother, pass the morphine the way

you did for Dad. Let me come, let me make a new home
in your heart, your good heart. Mother, I see you.

                     I finally see you.

CHARLES O. HARTMAN

Fathers' Sins

The slighted castle stood
for memory behind
our teeming neighborhood
and undermined

our faith in walls and keeps.
Those moon-benighted rooms
where old dishonor sleeps
in silvered tombs

we could leave sealed like dreams:
look out on our own ground;
take all for what it seems;
not turn around

E.K. PIGNOTTI

don't ask, don't tell

I. i don't think God was surprised when he learned
what i am.
i think he would have said,
should've saved that one
for later.

II. from Adam came Eve, so he was never a man
to begin with.

III. torn from the womb and thrust into Heaven's platoon.
our bodies aren't right
so it won't matter when they aim their muzzles
at our ugliest parts.

IV. we need more to replace the ones we've lost.
surgery will help.
quickly, stop the bleeding.
it's gone.
does she feel better now?

V. there is not enough white on your flag.
wave it higher. higher.
show them that you're not one of them
dig your heels in the dirt
deeper.
don't retreat, your body is your home now
raise the blade to your head
and bid your mother goodbye.

VI. does he feel better now?

VII. God didn't make me this way,
i did.
your stories are stupid.
all the crops & and stillness & the wind & the

spilled blood, a sower forsakes the seeds
and
hates.
Cain slaughtered Abel because
he envied his manhood.
but you don't see me killing my brother, do you?

VIII. your stories are stupid.
i read them anyway.
why do i have to fight?
lord, you handed me the gun
and you are surprised i squeezed the trigger.
why can't i know flowers and sunlight?

IX. on July 6, 1999, a soldier was murdered for loving a

X. i have no words.
all the words.
these ones.
we are out-numbered, but there are enough of us
to say
something.
which war is this again?
leave my name hanging like a fig
from God's lips
like he doesn't believe what he's saying.

ANTHONY WALTON

Frank Sinatra Reflects Upon Paris
on the Eve of the Sack of Troy

Tonight is the night
of your indiscretion,
so while some other
fool fills the jukebox
with dirty quarters
and the blues, you
get to choose—
will it be regret
or accusation?

The hollow hours
fill so slowly, sour
whiskey distilling
into futility. You
narrate your undoing,
star witness for the
prosecution, while
also serving in rebuttal
for the defense.
Was it your testimony
that you preferred
twilight to dawn—
or did you recollect
that it was all
in how you see it?

You can go home
with Hope or if you
prefer, her sister Dread—
or you can sleep alone
naked and rolling
all night between
the sheets of heat
and resignation.

ALLISON BLEVINS

Dark Matter

We should be concerned when scientists declare anything *mysterious*. A young girl named Vera grew up to solve the problem of invisible mass, matter that refuses to reflect or behave. I am a young girl in a hallway with my father, my daughter—12 and sharply focused behind him—watches. I don't know what he says, but I apologize.

Dark matter also exists in the human genome—non-coding regions with functions we don't yet understand, *enigmatic*—97% of sequences once considered junk. Imagine what answers wait.

Some of our days, I don't have words for the tears I can't control. You send flowers just in case—our marriage is built on the morsels between, everything unseen that shapes our physical universe—*gravity* and *motion* and *energy* no longer adhere to sense. How time moves slow but flashes swiftly in the looking back. How we are all tumbling toward a chaos we can't yet see.

WILLIAM WEBB

What happens at the table

Over and over
I am amazed about trust in marriage
my marriage my husband
26 days now I have sanitized our pizza board with alcohol
washed my hands until they are red
opened his PICC line and delivered
first a saline syringe
next the antibiotics
a saline syringe again
we go through 8 sanitizing packets each round
and I count to 15 (1 one thousand 2 one thousand 3 one thousand…)
25 time that is 615 numbers I have said out loud every afternoon
I am Philip Glass all day
counting off our rhythm like opera
on our stage
he swoons he catches he reclines he serves

I sing to Mike *breathe in breathe out breathe in*
when I push the syringe into the lumens
that lead to his superior vena cava
to bring down his infection
to heal his heart
superior vena cava

This is the most intimate we are all day
we sit leaning into each other
his pale upper arm given with exposed lines
my hands scrubbed clean and steady as I open swabs
and syringes
this is when we talk freely
and openly
I look into his eyes
as I push into him and he receives

WILLIAM WEBB

Orange Le Creuset Dutch Oven

I cooked in a Dutch oven
before I learned to cook
I was warmed over
many times in an unfamiliar kitchen
basted stirred and slowly heated
I was greedy to know everything about love

When he died
he did die as many did
in the 90's young and gay
I still visited the kitchen
and learned
Oh you know the list
kitchen and sorrow have comingled for years
grief basil anger tomatoes

Death interrupted my lessons
and I inherited this pot
because it was too heavy for anyone to lift alone
I carried it into my next home
For both of us

MARY LOU BUSCHI

Terminal Lucidity

The hospice nurse said she couldn't settle. Stopped talking or eating. I hadn't heard her say my name in weeks, confusing me with her sister, speaking Italian and getting frustrated when I didn't understand. Until a moment of mental clarity, the possessive pronoun, "my." On the last day, "my daughter." Hours before death, I made a chair out of my body—birthing position—to unmoor her.

A mother then to/a mother, a daughter/then never again.

JENNIFER JEAN

When is *fado* fate & when is it music?

Inside the Carrara marble,
a grave Mary, weighed by folds of fabric,
cradles her son.
His beard—flecked with thorns.
His murdered form—empty.
His flaccid face—agape. Another man, with a point
chisel & pumice,
kneels outside the stone block—eager
to find the pair & their luminosity.
As well, this man will find his name.

That is to say, *fado*

is both—always. The *BANG!* then, the force of fate
echoing across time: a first, blue lullaby
waiting to be hummed
into being
by the first Mother. & later, Amália Rodrigues
sings, *Fui bailar no meu batel…*
& we know this
plaintive vessel means
the beginning of all creation. The enemy
of chaos.

Letting Go

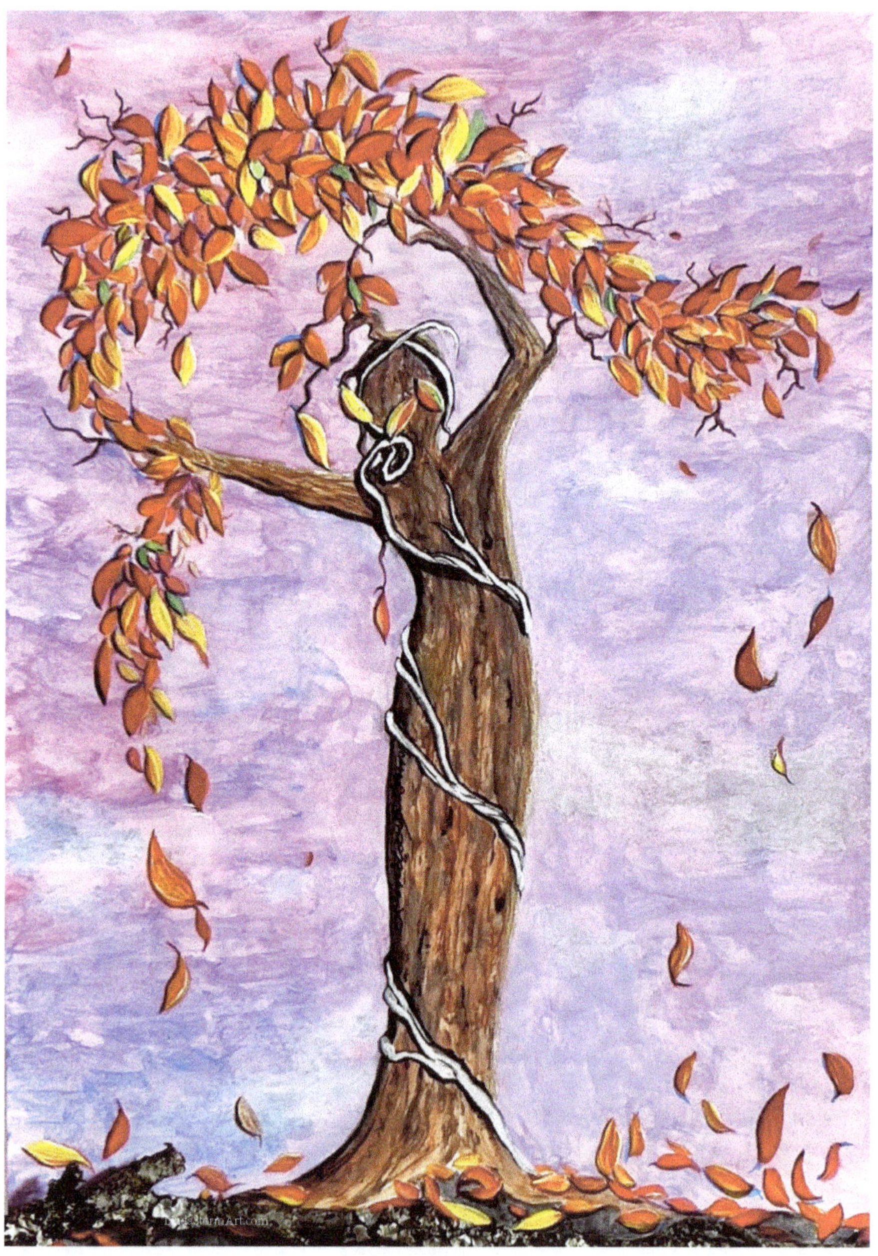

Poise

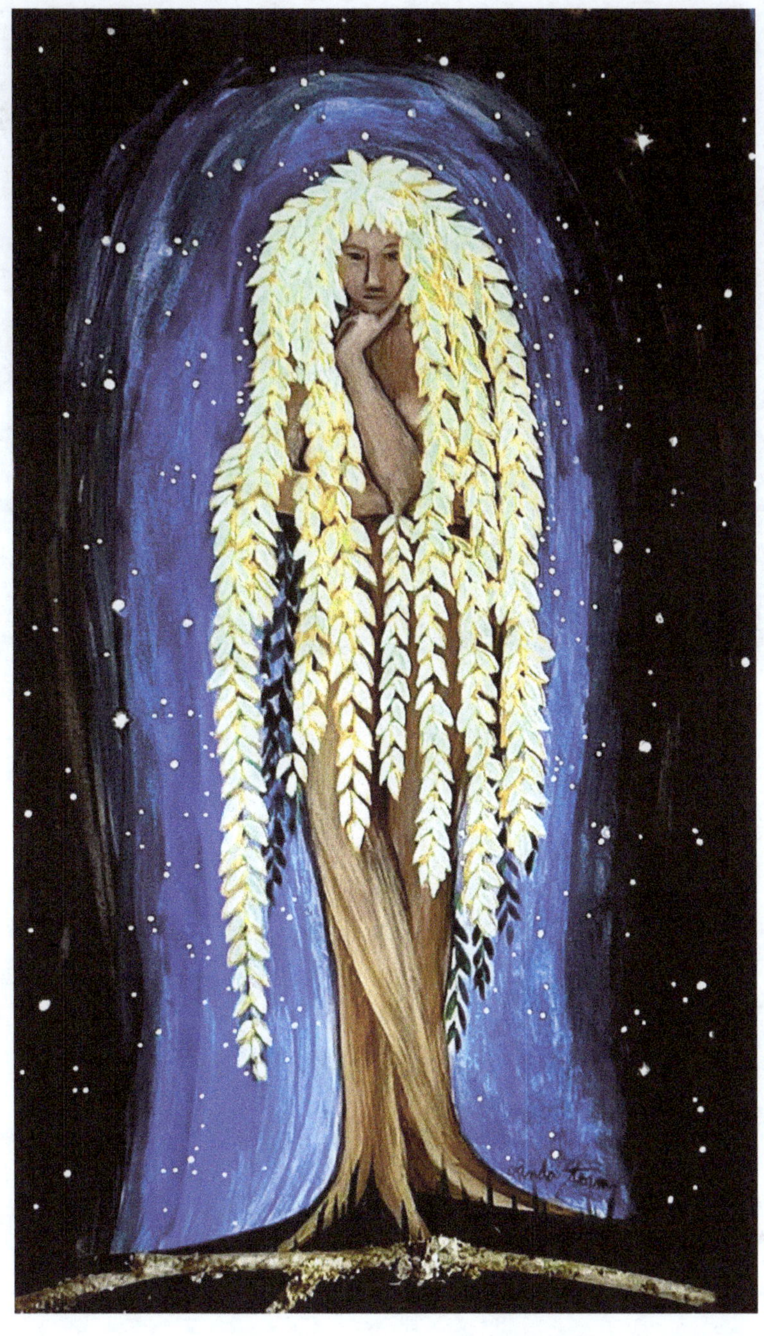

Tenacity

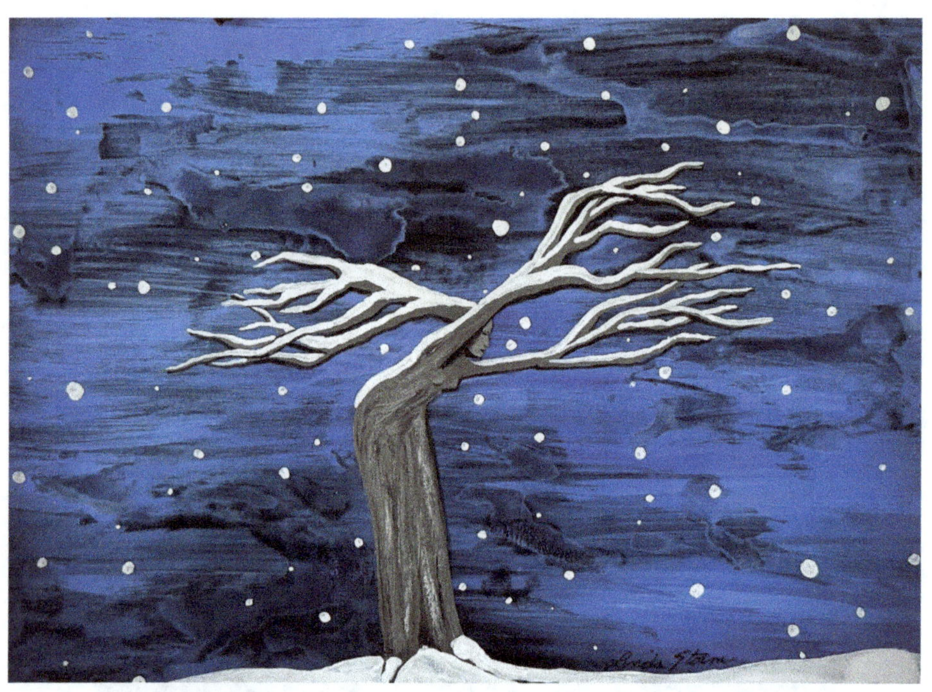

ALLISON JOSEPH

Aubade

Let there be caring light
        Let there be furtive light
Let there be ancient deliberate light
        Let there be lucidity, calm bathed in light
Let there be freedom to gather under lamppost light
        Let there be subtle strokes of sun in early light
Let there be no pain in the dawning light
        Let there be rising into good fortune, blessed light
Let there be humming, good cups, bright in morning light
        Let there be no secrets, clarity in incipient light—

ALLISON JOSEPH

Gratitude List in Late Middle Age

Grateful that the speck on the mammogram
was just a speck on the mammogram—

filthy little nodule in my upper left breast
biopsied into harmlessness. Grateful that

the blood of the month has sailed away
into oblivion, flashes in place of fear

of my body surprising me one clot
after another. Grateful that my back

isn't yet curled into a question mark,
that my knees are happy hinges,

neck still able to swivel away
from whatever I can't bear to see.

Grateful my vision is intact enough
to glimpse any stray neighborhood

bunny, high haunches peeking
above unshaven grass. Grateful

for these legs that still want to
leap from stone to stone on some

paved path I've wandered onto,
edged with roses someone else

had enough patience to grow,
nurture, hunger into being.

I'm grateful for hunger, for juice,
for the sizzle of fake bacon

in the morning, knuckle of butter
spread on sour dough to a thin

film, basic layer—I'm grateful
for breath and joints and lingerie
under my regular clothes, lace
over my scars, bold next to my

tattered shin, the rough shedding
and itch, scabs that dare not bleed.

CYNTHIA MANICK

On the NYC Subway I'm Asked,
"Where Is Your Smile?"

I say left it in my past life.

I say left it in bed this morning,
my hand a jack-in-the-box on snooze,
where I was having a good-
ass dream about buttered grits
and The Container Store.

I say I left it on a green bench
next to a guy who smelled like french
fries and the Mediterranean sea.

I say I left it at MOMA touring the exhibits.
It's walking past every red rope
mouthing titles and acrylic colors
like Prussian Blue.
It loves getting way too close to walls.

I say I left it wandering through Coney
Island on a weekday
sugared lips from funnel cake
long-boned fingers just right for cotton
candy and a Skee-Ball high score.

I say I left it next to a DJ stand at a roller rink
music a merry-go-round of bass.
It remembers a first kiss
with a boy and a lollipop mouth
where everything was a blossom,
and nothing was known about bills
or how a girl body curves
and tells the world something.

I say I left it in a memory of a school assembly—
rows of brown children like red-
winged blackbirds sing
O say, can you see and
the joy is a beehive at the
back of the throat.
Far removed from the KKK that's
recruiting now in Kentucky.

I say I left it in its first library—
drunk off pages where far away
places like Tahiti and
the boulangeries of Paris feel close.
It wants to live in language—
curl into the heartbeat of sentences
where vowels have no borders
no skin color
and every new name or combination
is a honeysuckle waterfall.

CYNTHIA MANICK

We Are Alive in Summer

Today the strawberry moon is blessed
by Chaka Kahn doing a meditation.
Blossoms shaped like stars surround her feet
and none of us notice the sun taking a bow.
Instead, we fall into Chaka's voice like ground-
hogs gorging on hibiscus leaves.
Do you remember your first real song?
How it sailed through black bottomed feet,
cut through muscle and went deeper?
It unspooled anything that needed a manual
for tenderness. Today we are alive in summer
and I am of two bodies – one filled with
honeyed fat cells, breath, acorn fibroids that
grow into a revolving ache. The other
chases words into poems filled with red
alder wood, a man's palm on the inside of
my left thigh, and watches the sky and sea roll
into the same shade of blue but doesn't want
to call it beautiful. That's such newborn phrase
for a divine thing that has a little darkness.
Today we are alive in summer and every
wanton berry is in season, strutting off roadside
carts. But all I want is sweet iced tea and clem-
entines. To remember the days of Saturday
morning cartoons, sound echoing off windowsills
when all the aunts and uncles were asleep.
A time when a smile was a word, words were
language, before a dagger became a bullet,
and a bullet meant someone's cousin wasn't
coming home. Listen. Today we are alive
in summer and I'm the last of the feral
children disguised as an adult. It's raining
again like the gods are cleaning up after a party.
I peel a rind like a gentle thing, carry a hum,
knowing this season can hold madness and light.

STEPHANIE BURT

Gingko

> *Plant gingko trees. —Angie Estes*

Famous for being ancient, forever
divided at the spine, their leaves' wings go
in all directions, then in the opposite
of those directions, purporting
to swing low, letting their wind-driven
flings show. What part can such superannuated
dwellers, spread out like the poles of a hammock or
sling, grow to play in this supposedly
new world? Though no human inspector, bunting, crow
or wren can tell which trees will bear fruit
before they do bear it, planners have learned to adorn
avenues with just one sex so as to block
the socks-and-cheese scent with which the trees' chartreuse
spheres, gathered like grapefruits on some
implausible string, mow
down pedestrians, while their nutritious
pits, fallen, solicit assiduous scavenging. Most days the privilege
of gathering, peeling, rinsing to take out
the sting, slow-
roasting and garnishing falls to old men, who tend
to Saran-Wrap their hands, thus avoiding the pulp
that would otherwise cling, dough-
like, to their fingers. All flesh
is grass. The so-called cycle
of life is a ring road,
trapping us in its sweet, otherwise
inaccessible center, where we regard ourselves
as green not-yet-ruined
reeds that can sing. O
stems, rootlets, cambium, sapwood that nobody
notices while you nourish us and fail to determine

our pronouns and whether we'll
drop what we make or keep at it till it's a missile we can
fling, so
far no one knows anything. You can water
us well or water us down or cut
us in half at the trunk and see what our
rings show. If you can't stand under
our odors, no wonder
you can't understand: we have become too old
to care what you supposedly civilized
dwellers, high-up in your own unaccountable, brittle
branches, even now all too ready
to see yourself as kings, know.

STEPHANIE BURT

Night Comes to Acton and Sudbury

Wide-eyed and hypervigilant, given—against all
              Evidence—her reputation
                      As wise, the pale barred owl
On this oak looks perfectly still, although her
              Irises and auricular muscles
                      Still move: she seems to scour
Schoolyard and sky as if awaiting, in the full
              Moon's light, the new moon,
Or the advent of some far owl-friendly nation.

All the tall bipeds seem to have fled indoors.
The parallel, thin suburban lanes are fossils,
              Trilobites, maybe, their ribs' arcs far
Enough apart for houses with lawns in between.
                      No other birds. No clouds. No stars
              As yet. We try to read the room.
The truth is great, we tell
              Ourselves, and will prevail,
Just not any time soon.

HEATHER TRESELER

Unmaking

It's Saturday—the first day without a bleating
alarm and early morning calisthenics
as we race past breakfast in our best buffed
skin suits for work and teleological life,
gunning the engines and our DNA spirals
for as far as our ruggedly fragile selves
might be pushed to travel.

It's Saturday, but we still make the bed, turning
the top sheet's rumpled edge like fresh paper
over a typewriter roll, and we try new scripts
in our unspooling heads: one of mutual
silence—or of light speculative gossip—
as we fish for the blanket down south,
wherever dreamland has kicked it.

It's Saturday, so we disguise, in neat sheathing,
the ark of our rest, place of our creaturely
coupling. Shyly, we curtain night's habitat:
lest there be tourist-peeping at the surprising
scene of last evening—that menagerie of bold zebra
desire and giraffe necking tower, those antic
wildebeests and florid midnight toucans.

It's Saturday, so we stow our wildlife under
a Calvinist spread and sham, hiding secrets'
sleep, our bodies' thirst and dram. *It's Saturday,*
your mute face seems to plead, *only one office is meant
to be busied*—as you catch me by the eye, loose belt,
untucked blouse, and shower-damp hair—
and unmake me again, properly, there.

DUSTIN BROOKSHIRE

Poem In Which I Proudly Have A Big Ole Ass

My ass is so bountiful, forget bouncing a quarter off it, bounce your first-born baby. My 5-inch inseam shorts are specially made to hold my scrumptious Georgia peach. My TikTok handle is @ThatBigOleGayAss. My hits are in the millions because I twerk. And I twerk. And I twerk. Did I tell you I twerk every chance I get? I also dance every time I hear Sir Mix A Lot's "Baby Got Back." is played. I tell anyone who will listen that I inspired that damn song—"Oh my God! Dustin! Look at *his* butt. It is so big. *He* looks like one of those rap guy's *boyfriends*. They only talk to him because *he* looks like a total prostitute." Homophobia stole my spotlight, so when I give a poetry reading, I request the podium be removed. I always recite this poem standing sideways, leaning into the mic so you can take in this big ole beautiful ass in all its glory before I walk off stage, letting your eyes feast.

DUSTIN BROOKSHIRE, DENISE DUHAMEL & BETH GYLYS

Scrooge McDuck Flipping The Bird Villanelle

A contoured villanelle using "Keep Them All" by Suzanne Allen

My bestie snorted, "Elon's ass was fired. He'd never quit."
He took his ketamine and caramel ice cream, both
fuel for his Scrooge McDuck fantasy: swimming in money.

He could fill Lake Erie with Franklins. And I was so broke
my wallet was empty, except for a pink slip. Trump is guilty
of being a little bitch. I hope he and Elon never quit

duking it out. My boyfriend's placing bets. I quit
following Musk and the bleach-bottle blond, his Valtrex bottles,
per Calser, under an alias—hiding is easy, he swims in money.

Surrounded by lackeys in a "yessir" environment,
Trump grew too fat, too sloppy, too maniacal, too
obsessed with holding a third term; he'll never quit,

lying, tariffing, shitting the bed and his diapers. You
and I are fired without cause. How can we stay
when politicians lead with hate, caring only about money?

We can't leave, though. Hell, we can't even afford lunch.
Elon is the world's richest duck. (I mean "fuck.) He's that
asshole, even when fired, doesn't stop spewing, doesn't quit
flipping the bird. He'll die alone, sucked dry by money.

LYNN McGEE

Maybe the Wrong Choices Taught Us
All the Right Lessons

Maybe I don't recognize faces out of context,
and come off not as I intend. Maybe I need

a break from human contact. I've even taught
my dog to be avoidant, to make a U-turn if there's

barking down the block — but secretly, we're both
drawn to the path of most resistance. Maybe this

has cost me a relationship or two. Maybe I'm not
known for my spontaneity, I watch too much TV,

and the only time I feel alive is when I'm weeping
at the feet of a well-told story, buzzed on wine or weed

or those first sweet lungfuls of humidity rising
from damp earth on a sunny hike, after a rain spell.

Maybe every forest is at risk of being deforested.
Maybe we're the last generation afforded the luxury

of denial while our planet absorbs damage,
steadfast as a woman who stays with her abuser,

afraid of losing her kids. Maybe I should have
had kids, maybe they would be here now,

looking at their phones and ignoring me.
Maybe I would know their faces anywhere.

DAVID GROFF

Happy Asteroid

Maybe it's aiming at us
if an asteroid can aim
or pick its point of pull
to make an asteroid of us,
earth its merger
and acquisition.
All of us all gone,
as done as dinosaurs.
I've told before

my sad sports metaphor:
my main death-fear
is to get left out,
chosen not last
for the team but not
chosen even last,
all the planet's players
pushing past my shade
to arena, course, or court
to make fresh records,
their next locker room
champagne shampoo,
their exclusionary win.

I ache to play and play,
to be in it when it ends—
game, set, match,
the stadium shut down,

or, to call it all a story,
to reach the last leaf,
the "The End" page,
the finale season in
our limited series,
its drama of combustion,

the likely stupid godless folly
of gotterdammerung.

I want us to go as one,
the whole damned team,
our ball a bouquet of fire
hurled to a shrinking universe
in one incendiary kiss.
To be together, all the time.
Asteroid, can you
make me happy?

DAVID GROFF

Stand

In the square they rally,
some in fury, everybody hurt.
I've stayed too far away for flags.
I can't discern the chant.
Government helicopters buzz us,
their whine and wind another menace.

I cannot manage all the murdered.
They keep contending, all the dead.
With their various bodies killed they say
look at us longer, no, linger, you,
choose us, be us, take our place,
whoever it is we are this week,

and they are right across their oceans,
even as the emerging domestic dead
and dying down the street demand
I look and be local, that my lament
extend and endure as a howl that will
amend the menaces, even as I know

our wrongs, our selfishness harken
way backward from this Friday,
a sunny day, cool to cold, full of fall,
9/11 weather, back beyond me
to every stupid cruel crusade
that gave my fathers bloody hands.

I feel too hard to enter the crowd
and open my arms to emend
the torrent of the toxified texts,
to turn lament into intention,

to move to clarify, call out
my chambered heart.

Standing here blocks away from it,
words not yet untangled in my throat,
I have to move it. I have to move.

PICHCHENDA BAO

Artist Statement During Wartime

My work is compromised.

My work is complicit.

My work is contradictory.

My work is contemporaneous with the ongoing violations of multiple

international treaties and agreements.

My work cannot keep up.

My work is thinking about sovereignty.

My work is thinking about autonomy.

My work walks around some talking points.

My work has never been on TV.

My work will never run for office.

My work cannot vote.

My work has nowhere to go.

My work digs in.

My work reaches out.

My work fails to communicate.

My work is unsatisfactory.

Still, it is necessary.

PICHCHENDA BAO

One Day, I Will Die

Let my memory be a blessing.
Let my blessing be a thorn
in the side of the empire.
Let it be sharp and painful.
Let it cause some real damage.
Let it leave an open wound.
Let nothing heal over it.
Let it weep and pucker and deform
the skin of the empire.
Let it let in every infection until the empire burns
with a fever that cannot be controlled.
Let it resist every intervention to remove it.
Let it course through the body of the empire.
Let it recruit the empire's own death.
Then, let it return to earth as dust
in the eye of the next empire.

LISA SULLIVAN

Interview with visual artist Millie Benson

In this issue of *Lily Poetry Review*, it is my pleasure to introduce to our readers the highly acclaimed Brooklyn, New York artist, Millie Benson. Ms. Benson's vibrant work has been exhibited throughout the United States and internationally. She holds a bachelor's degree from the Cleveland Institute of Art and a master's degree in fine arts from Hunter College. Millie manages private art collections and is a Senior Advisor to a private charitable foundation in New York City. She periodically curates art shows and maintains a studio in Brooklyn where she hosts various craft workshops for artists, makers, and musicians from all walks of life. To learn more about Millie Benson and view her work, visit her website at www.milliebenson.com.

Q: Thank you, Millie, for giving us a glimpse into your life as an artist. How and when did your interest in art begin?

A: My interest in art started around age 3 or 4. My mom worked at Greenville Museum of Art in Greenville, South Carolina. She would bring me to work with her. There was a Saturday class where we would draw and paint to music. The teacher would play Jimi Hendrix and a selection of classical music.

Q: Were you mentored or inspired by any specific artists?

A: My art teachers at Lakewood High School in Lakewood, Ohio were the first to inspire and mentor me. Mrs. Reboul would always say, "This is the best work you've ever done!" And it was true, because an artist is constantly evolving. Each creative action brings us closer to our full potential. I really can't say enough about the importance of having a great public school art teacher in America. So many wonderful teachers inspired me along the way.

At the Cleveland Institute of Art, my photography teacher Nancy McGintee was a strong influence. She was accepting and nonjudgmental of me and my work. These qualities were more common in the photo department teachers at CIA and desperately needed in the painting department staff! The painting program focused heavily on formalism and subjective elements were discouraged. In graduate school, Gabrielle Evers became a key influence. Her work explores the history and theory of color, which I studied both in undergrad and grad school. Color is a major part of everything I do.

Q: We are delighted to publish six of your works in this issue. I was immediately attracted to your sublime, celestial paintings and their complex colors, textures, energy, and auras. What prompted this series?

A: The series grew out of my fascination with the way in which humans image and imagine the universe. I've spent years working with long-exposure photography of the night sky, which led me to study astronomical imaging. I was looking at everything from Daguerre's 1839 crescent moon daguerreotype to the latest infrared and long-exposure images from the James Webb and Hubble telescopes. These technologies reveal phenomena beyond what the human eye can perceive from Earth. I became especially interested in the process scientists use to compile and translate layers of raw data into images humans can understand. The finished pictures are translations of the sublime and surreal qualities of astrophotography into a sort of painterly language of color and structure.

Ultimately, these paintings are about how we process vast, unknowable information through physical means. In a digital age, they offer a return to something primal and a way to feel our way through the cosmos we are discovering through new technology.

Q: I admire the geometric shapes in your paintings. To have something so structured amongst the abstract makes for an intriguing, evocative viewing experience. Why do you think you're drawn to geometric shapes in your art?

A: Geometry holds personal significance for me. My grandmother, my mother, and my aunts all sewed and made quilts. My aunt once told me she would plan quilt patterns in her head while cooking or doing dishes, letting the composition form in her imagination before ever touching fabric. I grew up sleeping under those quilts, dreaming underneath their structured patterns and stitched geometries. That memory of quiet, intuitive design and of geometry as care, creativity, and connection has a place within these paintings. It's the lived experience of how we conceptualize the abstract, how we bring vast, intangible ideas into literal perspective and our daily lives.

Q: Your paintings have some dramatic motion to them. Does this happen organically or is achieving that look intentional?

A: It's unintentional. In fact, there are times when I find it unsettling and almost ugly. It can feel chaotic or intrusive, especially when I'm aiming for stillness or control. But I've come to accept that movement is inevitable. Nothing truly stands still, and that's the reality of everything. So, I tend to follow the process, even when it leads somewhere unexpected.

Q: Let's talk technique. I understand you use long-exposure photography in your paintings. To the extent you are willing, could you tell us how this is incorporated? What other methods and techniques do you use: Spray, collage, drip, pour, pool, splatter?

A: The paintings are entirely process-driven. The idea is to push some basic tools to their extremes to reveal something new, create an unpredicted pattern, or to depict an idea or concept. I've developed a set of techniques that I pull from depending on what the painting needs. These include drawing and tracing to establish foundational gestures, spray painting and stenciling for layering and texture, and marbling with solvent-based, water-based, and acrylic paints to create fluid, organic patterns. I'll layer the marbled surfaces to build depth and variation, tape off shapes and colors to introduce structure and contrast, and use delicate hand-painting as well. And of course, color combinations are the foundation of all of it.

Long exposure photography is a way of pushing the camera to an extreme to capture something that can't be seen with bare eyes. This imagery goes on to inform color, shape, and composition choices within the paintings.

Q: Besides photography and painting, do you practice other forms of visual art?

A: I use collage, sculpture, and sewing as part of my process when they help map out ideas for a painting composition. Collage is a playful way to incorporate mundane subject matter into more surreal, fantastical arrangements. Sculpture comes into play when I'm thinking about how to represent weight or physical presence in a painting. When I'm considering human scale or tactility and how a work might feel or relate to the body, I sketch with elements of sewing.

Q: You have shared with us a wonderful photograph of your studio, which is chock full of various artworks and inspiration. I believe the painting shown on the table is *The Mothership*, published herein. On average, how long does it take you to complete such large paintings? In addition, could you describe how you begin a typical workday in your studio?

A: *The Mothership* took about one year from the first stencils and dips to the final layered detailed surface. Some paintings will get a few layers and then I'll leave them for up to 5 to 10 years and go back into them.

There's a joke about painters procrastinating where we say, "I'm cleaning the studio." Rather than face the blank canvas, I'll start a day in the studio by cleaning it. Once the studio is clean, I'll clean some more and organize some things. The result is that I've gently tricked myself into finally working on the paintings.

Q: Please tell our readers about your "embodied painting practice" and how that manifests in you and your artwork.

A: The act of standing in front of a painting and working on it feels like a form of time travel to me. I'm physically occupying the same space where a future viewer will one day stand. I think that the overlap between the artist's presence and the viewer's is one of the most intimate forms of communication we can have across time and space. It's a shared moment, even if we're separated by years and distance. That's what I mean by an embodied painting practice, my body, the gestures, the presence of me is part of the work, and part of the connection. It allows me to move backward and forward through time as well—when I'm wondering what someone will think of the work or when my old work looks totally different to me after the passage of time.

Q: When I view your paintings—I feel like I'm part of them—floating somewhere up in their universes, alone but not lonely, with colors swirling around me like gases. They evoke feelings of peace and wonder that I don't need to question, if that makes any sense. I imagine the environments are silent and cold but not bothersome. How do the paintings in this series make *you* feel?

A: Like I am at home. I feel seen and validated. They affirm something I've felt but couldn't articulate. The paintings feel like the walls of my home, and they are protective. Some are the size of a bed. A bed is for sleeping, dreaming, procreation, human evolution, development, hiding, healing. The paintings affirm all these human processes and experiences.

Q: I ask this question to many of the artists we publish because I'm fascinated by their varied answers: How do you know when your paintings are done?

A: A painting is done when the processes I'm using begin to converge and generate something new, something that doesn't fit with the rest

Q: I'd love to hear more about your "performative painting" experience. Your website lists "Selected Performances" and "Selected Discography." Are you a performer? Do tell!

A: When I was younger, I played guitar, bass, keyboards and sang in a few experimental bands. I like to make a lot of noise, the kind of noise that you feel in your body. I love writing, singing, and playing songs. I don't feel like someone needs to be a good player or singer to make a beautiful song. I don't feel like someone who can't draw can't make a beautiful image. If you find a way to express your idea in the clearest way and in its purest form, then that's enough.

Q: What is an interesting fact that we don't know about Millie Benson?

A: In my early thirties, I experienced a significant shift in my 20/20 vision due to a severe case of ophthalmic shingles, which resulted in the loss of most of the sight in my left eye. This change profoundly affected my studio practice and my perception of depth and visual rhythm. I now see only blurbs of light through one eye and clear detail through the other, a contrast that has reshaped how I think about the physical balance of my body as I move through space and about the visual balance of my paintings.

Q: What would you say has been the highlight of your career as an artist
thus far?

A: The highlight of my career was during the early years of my son's life,
while I was working full-time and navigating new motherhood. Despite limited
time and no external demand for my work, I committed more deeply to my
painting practice than I ever had before, which flew in the face of everything
I had been taught. I'm of a generation of artists where the prevailing narrative
was that you had to choose between motherhood and your work. The period
immediately after my son was born marked a turning point in taking myself
much more seriously as a professional artist.

Q: Lastly, what hard-earned advice would you give to budding artists?

A: Take care of yourself, your body, your soul. Be kind to yourself. Treat
yourself to the luxury of time. Take the time you need for your process and
then take even more time.

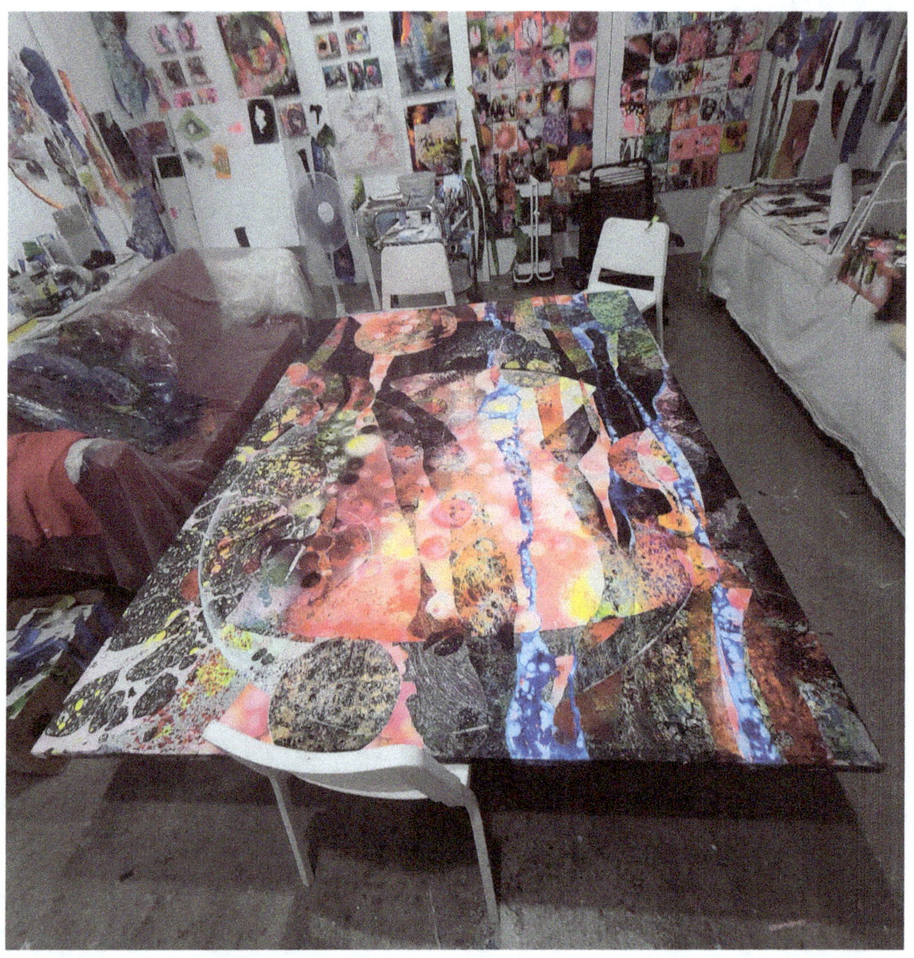

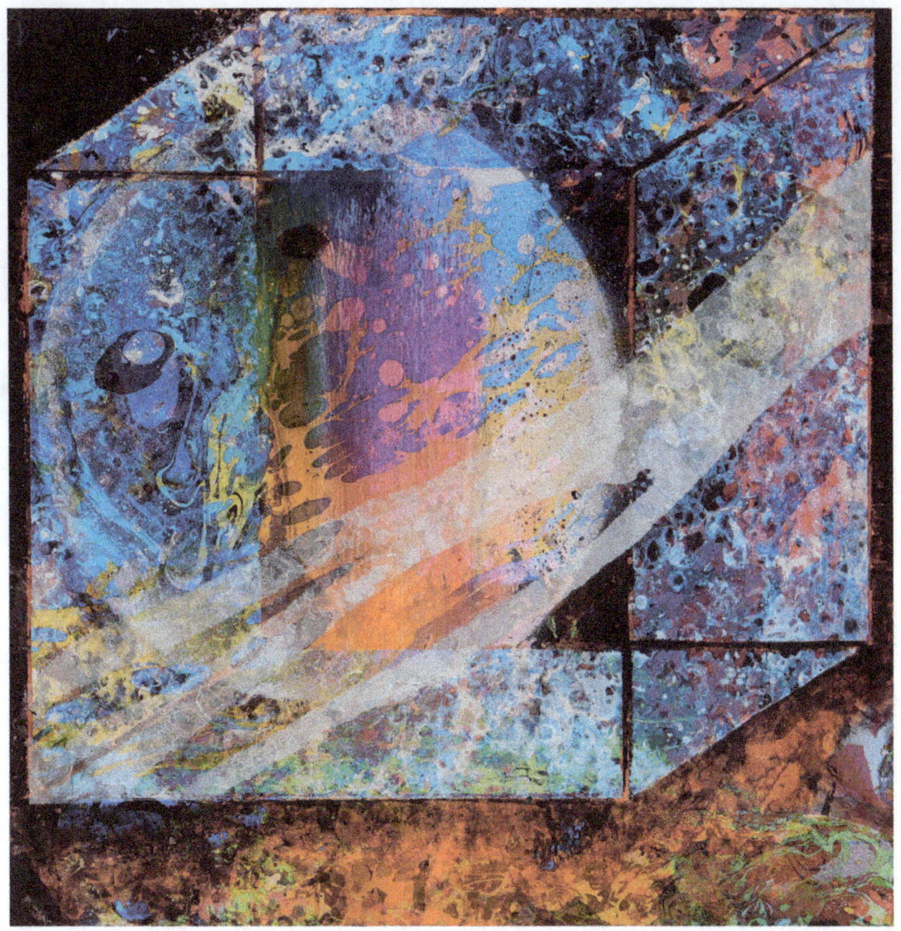

Tumbling Lace Moons

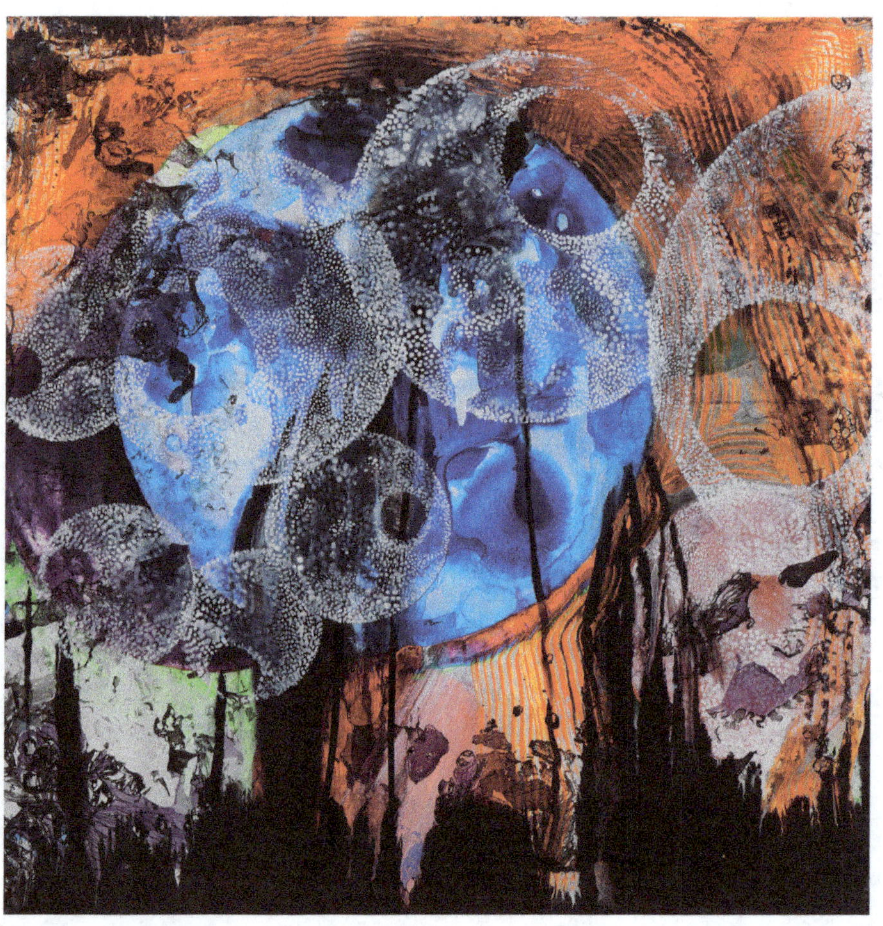

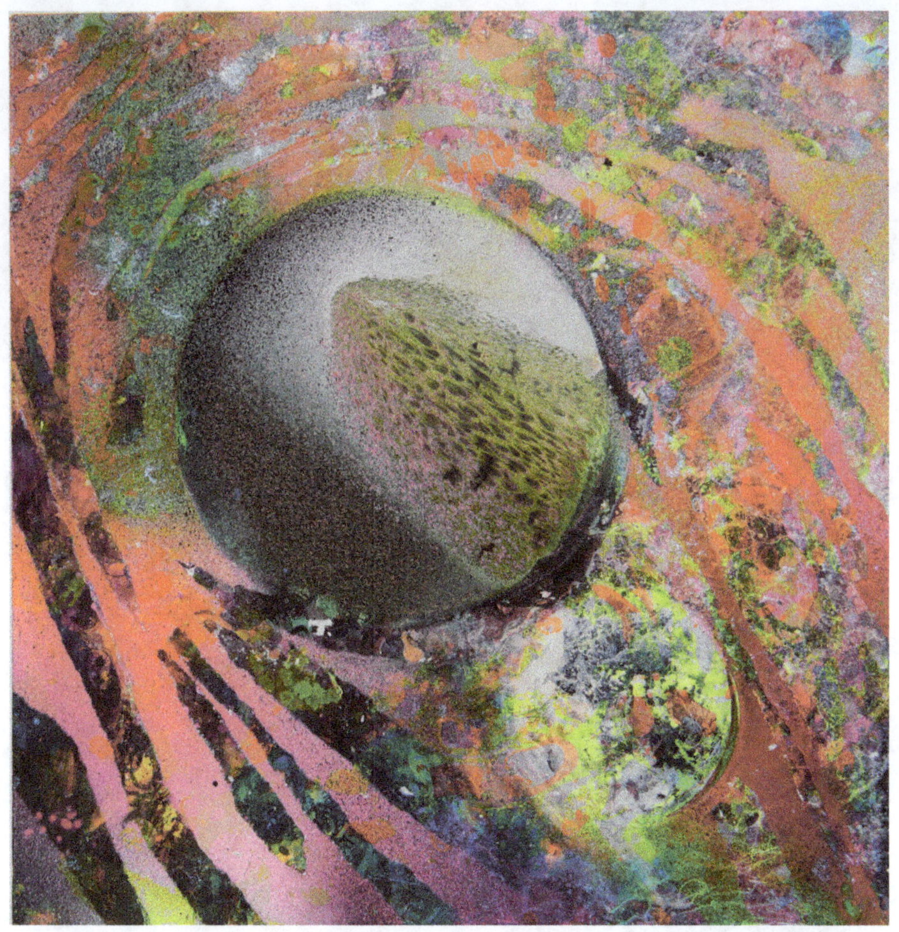

The Mothership

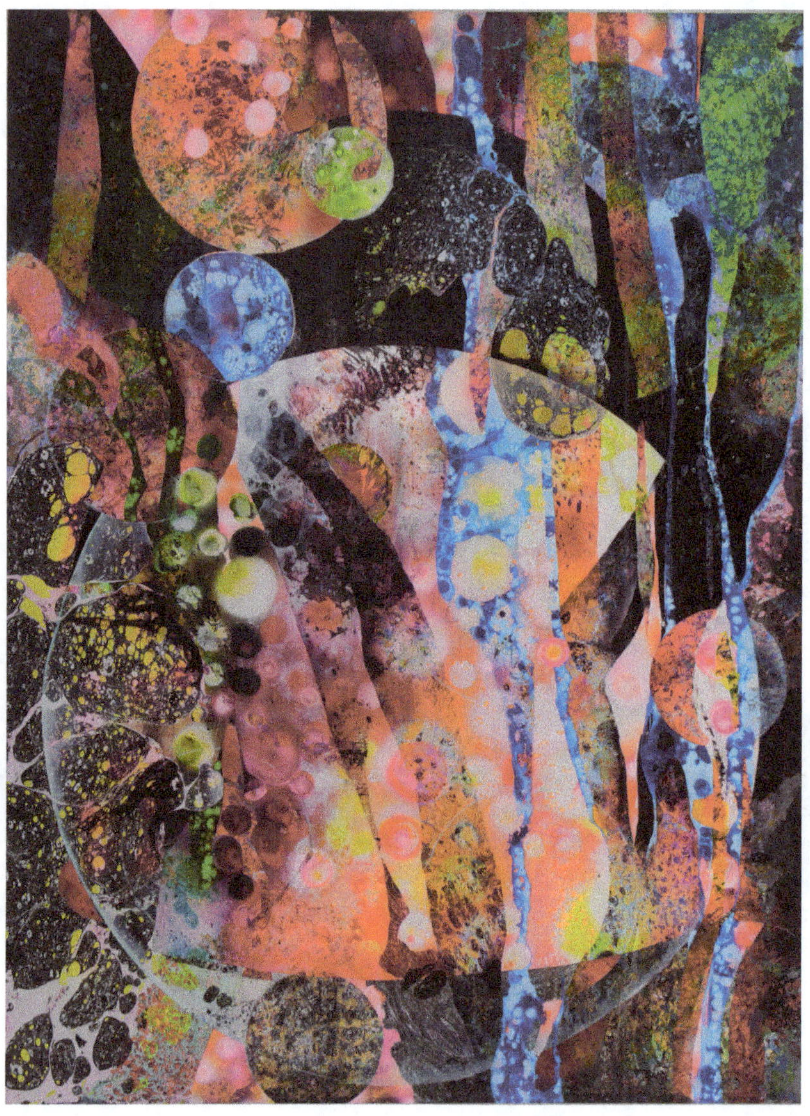

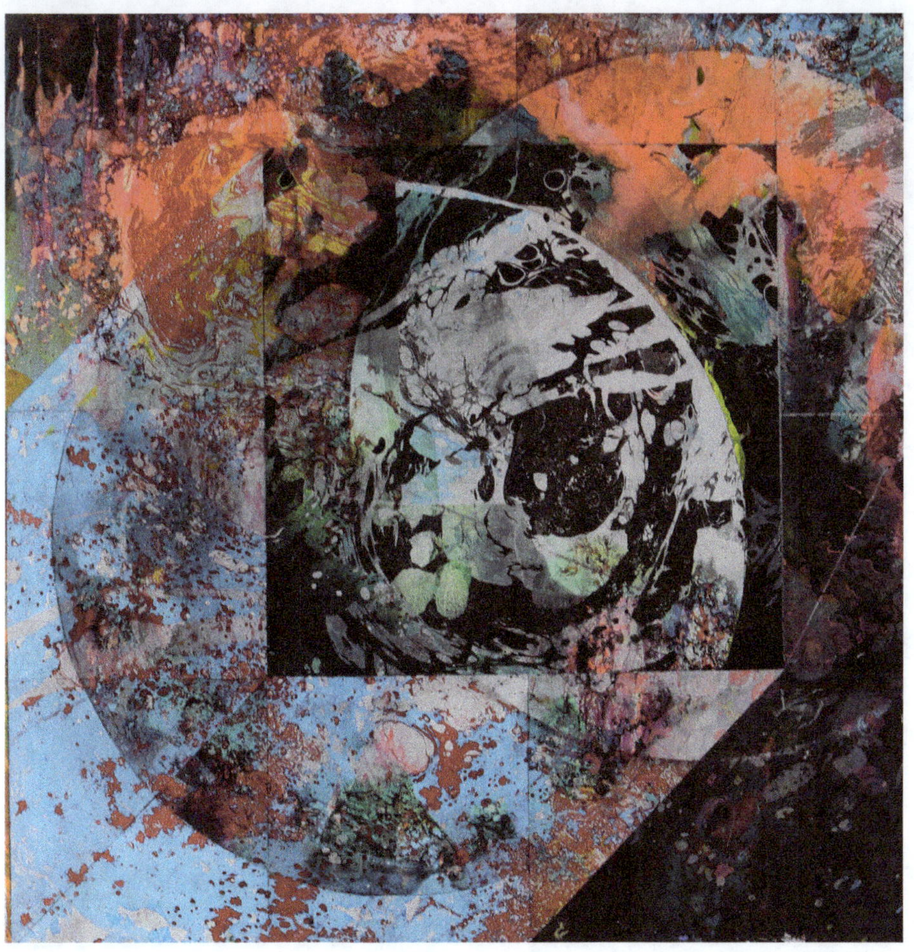

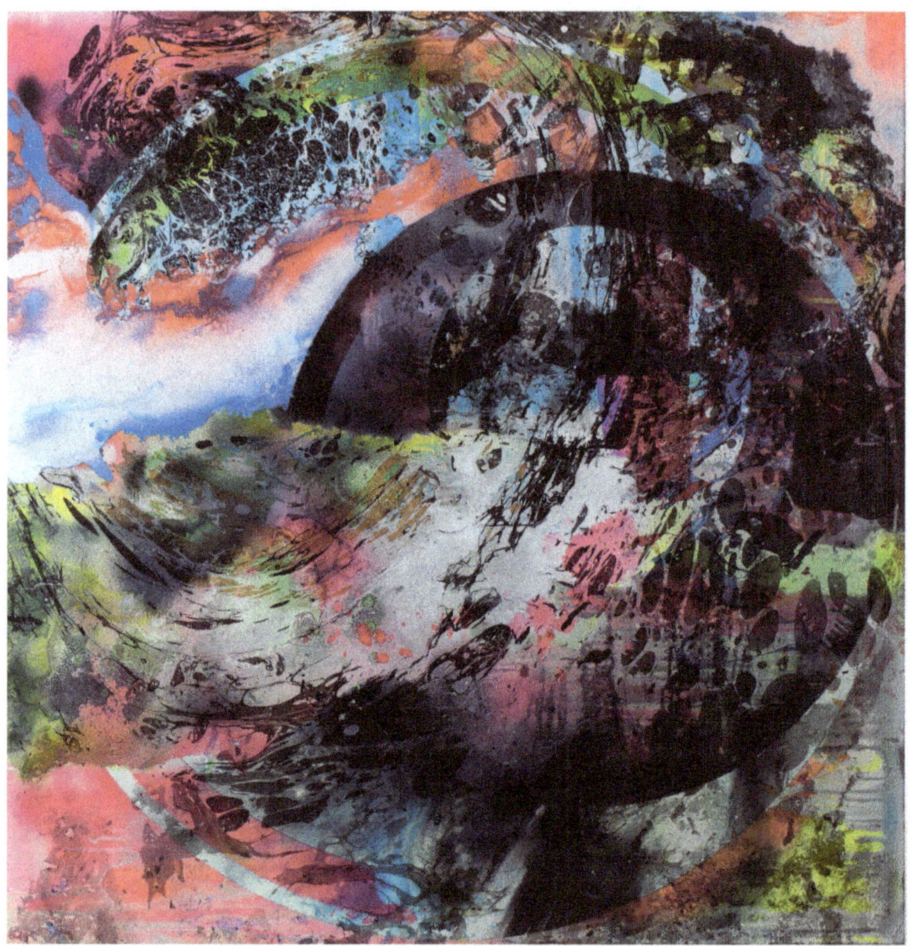

JARED HARÉL

Too Young to Be Left Alone,

my grandma took me with her
to the public toilet.

And maybe because I recall
so little from that age,

I cannot forget
standing in the stall

and her seated, suddenly
my height. The walls

were beige, floor green.
I had never seen

so much skin in my life.
I knew almost nothing

but can still picture
her slumped handbag,

those hidden folds,
and how my grandma, lost

in some everyday thought,
sighed before she

finished and flushed.

JARED HARÉL

Debt

The man that owed my dad money
died owing my dad money.
To be honest, the whole thing
was depressing as hell.
Dad went so far
as to visit him in the hospital;
held his clammy hand
beside the arithmetic of machines.
Naïve, Dad believed the man
might pay back a decent lender
before a scary one,
or that he'd bother at all
with the end-game so near.
Not a prayer, I laughed, when sunk
into his sofa, Dad asked,
So you think I'll ever get it back?
I feel bad about that now: my answer
like a verdict, a diagnosis, a death.
How I too keep defaulting
on my debts to him,
and how it nearly never pays
to be gracious or good.

JP HOWARD

List Poem or Alternative Words to Describe Mama

Mommy, Moms, Mother,
Diva, Leo lady, Spotlight,
Sad, functional alcoholic, Gorgeous,
Outgoing, Introvert,
Restaurant aficionado,
Lady who never learned to cook,
Lover of Sarah Vaughan, Dinah Washington,
Billie Holiday, and all things jazz
Drinker of Smirnoff and smoker of Salem menthols,
from Friday night into the weekend
Runway model, lady who strutted her stuff,
Court clerk for 45 years,
High school graduate,
Renowned bachelorette,
Except for the few years you were married to Daddy,
Giver of no fucks,
Sometimes fucked up from all that life dished out,
Depressed, suicidal, pill popper,
Suicide survivor,
Deeply spiritual,
Believer in God,
Print model,
Magazine cover girl,
Daughter of Pearl,
Mother of Juliet,
Lover of Drama,
Sometimes selfish,
Selfless, Generous,
Voracious reader,
Only Child,
Reluctant adult,
World Traveler,
Sugar Hill, Harlem's favorite Diva,
Mama!

JP HOWARD

Haibun Love Note for my NaPoMo Poets

We write in circles. Our poems sustain. Some days we sexy muthafu-kas. Other nights we memory and nostalgia. We hold worlds in these words. We hold each other up. Our poems are in conversation with one another. We write across race, religion, age and sexuality. We melting pot. We sacred space. We praise poem. We anti-praise poem. We whatever the fuck we want to be. We poetry church. We amen and hallelujah. We haiku, haibun, tanka, etheree, sonnet and eintou. We new forms and ancient forms. We prose poems and narrative poems. We storytellers. We each other's reflection. We joy. We sad. We open palms. We fist full. We scream. We whisper. We past and present. We so fine. We so fire. Sometime we ice too. When April goes, what we gonna do?

We write together
Everyday we unwrap gifts
Between our stanzas

JESSICA L. WALSH

Pasture

Moving bins shadow me
instead of chattering students

who dart from my classrooms,
heads bowed to phones—

Do you know about wonder?
I say to their desks.

How an ode lit my nerves
and tremored my hands

until the professor frowned
and offered me a cigarette—

Virginia Slims menthol,
for the irony—

then looked away,
embarrassed for me.

How I read an elegy
sun-sleepy on the quad

and fell into my own death,
the truth of my death,

my classmates' light joy
like another language

as I saw the blanks of my epitaph
for what they never asked.

How even here, in my first years,
I pinched back tears at a line,

felt my spine crackle with it,
whatever it was—a fog of embers.

Yes, I was a fool to follow wonder
when there were other ways to live.

To chase it is to live alone on a planet
of real gardens and dead toads.

Solitude adopted me
and my violence of feeling.

My audience has always been
an empty room.

JESSICA L. WALSH

Pretty Life

Every woman I talk to
wants a way out of her pretty life,
though lately I don't talk to many people,
mostly my dad who is dead
and the picture of a friend
who went the painkiller route
and off all grids,
moved to a farm of all things,
and I say to her picture,
what the fuck, girlie,
are you doing there,
how did it happen—

Every woman wants—
I want to say—
this is a good life, I love my people
and I'm dying to get out of here,
no one's princess in a tower
just a hag in a mop closet,
Bitch Radley,
asking myself
what the fuck, girlie,
are you doing here,
how did this happen.

YERRA SUGARMAN

I Want to Know the Part of You that has No Name

I want to know the part of you that has no name, the part
that takes refuge in your territory of blood and muscle.

I want to touch her tear-salt and her hollows.

Tell me how to find her: the you who despairs into song,
then turns notes into seeds of light.

The part who combs the nighttime in my hair silently falling.

Is there anger in her sentences? The taste of earth on her lips?

May she repair the world with hands that strike the heart in prayer.
May she polish each day as if it were tarnished silver.
May the color in her eyes blossom.

CONNIE POST

Entomology Lesson

I am curious about a bug
that's been in my kitchen
for three days

I look at hundreds of photos
on google

I compare body colors
and wings
and wonder why
I can't just
pick it up
and let it outside

I step carefully across
the slanted patterns
of light

I am always listening
for the heavy footsteps
of dusk

I am praying to
an atheist sky

I watch the
merciless moon
ever present and inebriated

I watch this insect
day after day

and every time
it scampers away
I remember the way

we used to scatter
to the darkest corners
of the house
when my father came home

SUZANNE FRISCHKORN

Cusp

(after A.R.)

I prefer to leave the map, the knife,

  where they belong,

buried in the trunk of a childhood home.

   I labored too long

to part clouds and see sky.

   I'm waiting for buds

to green gnarled branches.

   I don't want to recount

the steps I took to arrive.

   My time, limited. I know what I know.

I hear Persephone's light footfall in the hall.

ROBIN DAVIDSON

The Hidden Mother

How to keep a child still, that was the problem in early photography.

The seated child enduring the long wait for light

to expose an image on silver-plated copper.

In Victorian portrait studios women hid behind red velvet couches,

wingback rosewood chairs, wound their heads and hair

in sheets, draped themselves in curtain fabric

or dark-colored quilts to conceal their faces and necks and arms,

until all that remained was the shrouded former self.

The apparition of mother, soothing the small

body before her, the wriggling child quieted by invisible hands

until an image could appear. Not so much otherworldly,

as the haunting knowledge of a mother's

future vanishing. My mother too was a present absence,

and I, the still child, waiting to be seen.

Only now do I know what it means

to remain hidden, to let oneself become a ghost,

so another might have palpable presence

in the world.

ROBIN DAVIDSON

Questions for Lee Miller

You tracked mud and ash from Buchenwald and Dachau into the room,

then stripped naked to pose for the camera like an empress

in Hitler's empty bathtub to bathe away a war's filth.

Your boots in the foreground, the victor's.

What memories are mirrored in the body's raw presence?

Exposed, exposure. Blond hair, blond back, poised for the Zeiss lens,

the eye of the father, the Führer. How many are shamed

in the gazing? A brute's a dictator in any household.

You look out at me. I look back at you. We both know who's who.

I could not bear Auschwitz as a tourist. You could not turn away,

marked by seeing, being seen. Photographs insist, cancel time

and death, a black-and-white membrane between worlds.

Can you hear me? Can you help me part this veil between us?

The sun's setting through the cedars now. It's evening and cold.

JOANNA SOLFRIAN

Hold and Wyatt

A storm is coming tomorrow. The storm
has already arrived. One will have pure white
flakes, the other pure white desires.

We go on draining pasta, loading the dishwasher.
My friend, a retired colonel, says, "everyone knows
fight or flight, but there's also hold."

I am holding a cup of coffee. I am holding a pencil.
Yesterday the car held my child and her friend;
the highway held the three of us.

The "great criers" of the last wars are dead.
Graves, Akhmatova, Merwin—the point was
we were supposed to *heed* them!

I wake early this morning to the call of a bird.
In the near-dark, I can't tell what kind—
but the call, insistent, unanswered, is familiar.

There is still love, which grows from almost nothing.
Over Zoom, my student interrupts an inequality problem
and says, "That's my dad calling—let me hold you."

Then last night, on the drive, the getting-to-know-you: twin brother,
older sister, dad felled by a brain tumor. From the back seat
the boy said, "I'm starting to forget what he sounded like."

PHILIP F. CLARK

Benediction (On a portrait by Bill Brandt)

Startled, she unbends and stops her cleaning; looks at us,

her eyes are cautious questions. We have stopped her work.

The light is a warm thin cut on her lips.

She wears a wedding band, a kerchief, her dress is torn in three places.

The stone floor has calloused her knees,

wet where she has washed it. Is it her home,

or that of another -- some family she works for?

Is she a maid or a mother?

Her brow sweats and yet she's smiling,

looking past us, or past this life, to the life ahead.

It is mid-day but dark, the sudden streak of sun on her

another feeble interruption. There is so much to be done.

In a moment she will go back to her work;

she will make the house clean, she will

drink something perhaps, or start dinner

for a husband perhaps, and children.

Alone in the room

of someone else's house

she will think of things that are new and clean:

a life, a dress.

PHILIP F. CLARK

Illumination

In this warren of our bed,
my hands are useless, I have no cincture
for the dark on your rough belly.

Like a famished lamp, bereft of moths and empty
of fire, my eyes are the brighter flame on you,
after our wine-fed evening.

There are other thirsts in this masked world;
I have heard mouths learning a new language.
Hands and lips pay obeisance.

I barter for a dowry of affection;
the least of it a frail banter
over this sleeping flesh.

Age has carved its lessons in us.
I would have it no other way
if only to know the heft of you now:

Arm and leg, the neck and clavicle
I know so well. I recognize desire.
But the lexicon is lost. Memory fills with ash.

I trick the dark into speaking.
My mouth to yours, I illumine all the risk,
Knowing that touch has its cautions.

PHILIP F. CLARK

Genuflection

I was too early.

She did not see me walk in,

or hear the door open,

and at first I did not see her.

Slowly, three times, she knelt on one knee, three times

she crossed her chest, there

in the small triangle of a corner

in our old kitchen.

I thought perhaps I'd misconstrued

her gestures.

In an instant, I knew.

When our eyes met, she was not there.

Believe me, I have imagined wrestling angels;

I have seen Giotto's Lamentation — those upraised arms

on one of them, stretching in grief among an unresponsive sky,

wondering, 'How'? 'How?' 'Why?'

Between the fill of tears, and an uninvited laugh

I tried, too, to see what she was looking at

in her sudden church.

Rage or tears or curses, none of these would do.

I went to her slowly, knelt too. 'Mom, come sit,'

and I raised her bird-small arms. I walked her

to the living room, her shaking figure bending to rest.

She kept looking away.

What does one do? One accepts.

I never remembered prayers

but some lost fragments of one came to me.

It had something to do with saints.

The nurse would come in a few hours.

I could wait, not speak, just listen. I could learn

to have some faith.

JENNIFER MARTELLI

After: Iris Maria Tusa's "Presence of Absence"

Are you able to leave a place that, at one time, let you in? How long would you stay after your welcome has been revoked? And how would you know? When did you stop reading signs?

*

Reader, I ask myself these questions every day. Every day of my life.

*

I've been told, also, never to use the word "murmuration" in a poem.

*

Never speak of the flock's leaving and returning to the roost after a good feed; the rustle of a thousand pair of wings.

*

The singularity of thought in a collective mind. The collective mind sending dreams and panics through the night.

*

My sponsor says that my belief in (and fear of) exclusion is simply another way of hurting myself: addictive as a line of cocaine, smooth as my menthol cigarettes, sharp as a steel hook, repetitive as birds migrating and feeding. She says, *this serves you in some odd way.*

*

My husband asks me, *How many times are you going to watch this same film?* I tell him, *A thousand pairs of wings.*

*

In the film, young women audition, are accepted—or not—to a dance
company run by witches. They soon read each other's minds. I think, would
my daughter be let in? Would I want her to be there? No matter what hap-
pened in this brutalist building?

*

No matter the danger. The murmurs in the walls. The gutting hooks, sharp as
a goat's antler, as the thin claw of a bird.

*

I mean, who doesn't want to be the hands of a flock, the sex of a murder, the
heart of a coven?

*

Who hasn't watched their child excluded and knew nothing had ever changed?
That the fear of exclusion is as old as the fear of God.

*

A flock lifts from a roof. Lifts, forms a spiral, a cloud, almost lands, moves off
like a plague. As one thought. A bird is left in the eave.

JENNIFER MARTELLI

Corsets

Mother wants us / back beside her—Thom Yorke, *Suspirium*

They are like molting pythons because they constrict.

They are like lactating mothers because they hug.

Because corsets insist, they are a ballet position that wants you erect.

They smell as you do: their plaster and fabric thirsty for your sweat and,

except for your mother, corsets know you best. Their bones stay

the pain of standing too long. In their corset greed, they want

to take you in and close the open spaces with their metal buckles.

In this way, they are like homes we've all lived in, homes

with drafty windows and old horsehair walls.

Corsets are molded to your every breath and without them,

you could not stand, not for a minute, not with all your pain

and brokenness, you could not stand upright, in your clothes.

JAN FREEMAN

Cat's Cradle

 I wove a cat's cradle in a house of string
The beautiful rooms were simmering
while a chicken cooked in a shallow brook
I spat a red clot from a cut with her diamond ring

A friend arrived with a buttercup
Hold it under your chin with a pin, she said
She opened her mouth and the house fell in
Each simmering room disappeared like a cat

If I rinse my mind with a bottle of bleach
if I scrub my chicken and boil my screech
if I walk on the river to the bridge with a view
if I sit on its edge and chant the clues, who cares?

The rain will fall like dew if I do
the chorus of cousins will boo if I do
the string will hang me whole if I do
and the red clot cut in two will flood if I do

Will I keep my buttercup mouth pinned shut
will I open it up like a jack-in-the-box
will I live or die in his murderous eye
if I tell the truth? Will you?

LEE BRICCETTI

Reading Milton: Unparadised (Do Not Resuscitate)

> *...couple linked in happy nuptial league,*
> *Alone as they.*
> —John Milton, *Paradise Lost*

Together they. They, with weary countenance.
A few bouts of irritation may also be fond company.

He. Still that dazzle of sulk & curls.
She. Fugue behind her ear. Headache & chest pain.

Childhood, ever did she have?—pulled full-grown
from his Mother-bone, his laugh & slouch, his paunch

& cock. She. Heart valve newly replaced. Plastic
thread trussing her torso.   Together, they. They,

a few ripping fights. DNR on the fridge.
Yet, it had been, or it still was good—sitting,

touching. To cook an exquisite meal
is better than sex now, she said, hurting him.

He, wincing. Smiled at his child bride. They.
Red wine, ossobuco. Very-Paradise.

PHILIP MEMMER

Excerpts from *Boatman*

             There where you were

And here between   not much at
                      all:
             defining other

        whose lives felt like stories

          the gods implored me
like it matters
         And does it I asked

    Anything   they said again

There where you'll be

the faintest of lines
from other
                But for you
well…
        Come up with something
Anything   *Make them feel*

the shallows cold on my heels

Just make them feel anything

        Boatman they call me   though   once   never once have I ever
                              never   never honestly even
                    given a name
              said hel-
lo   they say
                                              the river wide
                          Hello   nothing they could return to

        behind me   behind them   the craft   appears to us both

            And right on time   and we go
in whatever way they imagine it should   we should go

        however they imagine

There's no fare   no fee
                              You've paid   everything you had

                    So enough with the coins   on your tongues   and on your
                                                  eyes
          Where exactly would I spend them
                                                  and on what
                              And no entourage
                  enlisted to voyage with you   no horses or cats or soldiers

                  the ticket you were born holding   We'll go alone
                                                        folded in your fist
          How could I sell you   the one thing

                                                        you've always owned

ALAN FELSENTHAL

The Greats Going Away

the rack of time is shrewd
like gas smells

from behind a closed door

the pilot light blown out
by the wind through
a cracked window

not broken

open

ALAN FELSENTHAL

Arm Yourself with Clairvoyance

the ninth and final stage

a soul must pass

freightless

cosmic balance

signing heavens seven

our ancestor the hexagon

then limbs, a head

before the hub

of death-birth-life

diaphanous curtain

lone sunblink

to say what

D. NURKSE

A Night In Mercy

The head nurse said, *back in a sec.*
I lay flinching. That ward was empty.
The operation was a blank.
I stared as if my eyes
could grant a future, but no,
just volunteers pushing carts
silent as time on rubber wheels.
At last a cough at the open curtain.

The master surgeon, Rolex
in the room, Nikes in the corridor.
His gesture, wrists revolving
around a fixed point, meant
wrap it up. So I turned to the wall
and waited for time itself,
pure sequence, and after midnight
an old man limped in to water the coleus.

How will I pee? I asked.
He lowered himself in stages
onto the edge of the bed and told me.
How will I eat? How will I sleep?
How will I know I am dreaming?

He thought. I sensed he yearned
to glance at the clock whose second hand
advanced in saccades. But he continued.
If he came to a part he didn't know, he said so.

How will I know how to be loved?
What about the cruelty of desire?
What about the wind that blows us away?

When there were no words
the orderly showed me with gestures.

The air between his open palms
began to quicken and hesitate-—

there, outside, beyond the double panes,
in our exhausted city, dawn had come
and the hypnotic signs were fading.

D. NURKSE

Another Country

I loved the dog so much I wanted him
to live far away, in another country,
where another owner would be responsible
if he cut a pad on glass, choked on acorns,
or just ran free in the tall foggy pines
too happy to ever return: let someone else
pry a blood tick from his matted croup,
soak the kibble for toothless old age,
coax buckling hind legs: let a stranger
wake long before dawn, in the dark
of an endless windy night, and listen
for the catch in that soft adamant breath.

D. NURKSE

The Hunters

No sooner had I died than I met them:
a party of five with a mad-eyed dog
in the birch forest north of Sunderland.

One had an ammo belt. One was just a child-–
I almost smiled at his wisp of moustache.
Two at the rear carried a pole
on which a young deer was slung.

"So you can kill even here?" I asked.
The leader put a finger to his lips.

I was new to death: the beauty of those hills,
and their silence, could still destroy me.

ANTON YAKOVLEV

Trauma

But in truth, nothing is killing you,
chandelier on fire. You give better light than a saint's
relics. Your next ten years are Apollo,
an icebreaker in spite of fascism.
I know the pinball tilt of your head,
the documentation of your anger.
Pulled by a rabid horse, the carriage gets there first,
so what good would it do to heal?

You stood on the bridge as it opened.
The sail of a passing ship
caught your pant leg, and off you went
into the harbor, hanging onto the mast.
Only a fool or a villain would cut you down,
make you tumble down into the trench.
Dear friend, let your wound water your legacy.
No invading soldier can stomp it out.

I look in your rearview mirror to brush my hair,
growing smaller in your steady advance:
streaks of gray on my head,
late night visits just to refrain from words.
Floorboards creak like a religious schism.
Papagena's biopic blew up the projector.
Now we only fail to destroy each other
when we actively wait to die.

SEAN THOMAS DOUGHERTY

Orchids

(Golden Shovel with lines from Jean Valentine's "Fidelities")

Once I was in a white room. Your
Hands are a white room,

One I want to be. To be. There
Are places like a womb. This

Winter when the white
Wind bandages the world like a room

One we walk through, or like books
Without words, pages of papers

That turn as we become the letters
Wind-blown, blowsy. We put stamps

On our bodies, mail them return. We name the
Brethren. Once long ago a pay telephone

Rang on a corner. I answered it. I heard *"Our
Love is a ember as are our lives.*

Then the line went dead. We
Wander this earth weary till we are

Awakened. By the river, Always
You are the one I am choosing

Hand by clenched hand. Our
Fists unfurl. We let go our lives—

PAGE HILL STARZINGER

Here

In my seventh decade,
the ice caps melt so
quickly that earth's rotation
slows and to adjust we
add leap seconds into
the clock. In my seventh
decade, I pour the oil
of flowers and herbs
down my back, because
my skin dries out like the
ground remaindered after
we pump the water
table too low. Wild fires
scorch the west
and sex becomes virtual.
My cats watch birds
online that may not
be alive anymore. They
may even be extinct.
In my seventh decade,
the doctor says,
Hope is the magic bullet.
Does this beg the question
of pattern. I worked
for a long time in a
world in which we
followed seams around
the body. Bias-cut was
the term and everything
flowed. In my seventh
decade, a twenty-year old
says, don't worry, the water-
bears will inherit the
earth. If this is adaptive
behavior, I'm not here
for it.

BARBARA UNGAR

Portage

I've lost my calendar   but found my passport
        wherein I look like a weary felon

        (with my first passport   stamped around the world
        I frolicked like Bambi)

Earth's on fire 73% of wildlife gone
        Man is in the forest

Children burning too   before our eyes
        on our phones

        I'm somewhere between   asking for
        those little anodynes

        that deaden suffering   and
        and then to go to sleep)

The cosmos is 80% empty   voids
        brimming with cosmic energy

yet I cling to this illusion   of an I
        a blossom withering

Yours   the sudden blow
        I still stagger under

KELLI RUSSELL AGODON

After I Read Your Self-Elegies, I Think How Unfair the World Is

for Marty

I understand you're trembling, no longer

waltzing, the years you ran the stairs

by your house, did pushups at the top.

Remember that residency where we toasted

Berryman from the edge of a cliff, tipsy

and in love with the stars? We believed

we saw a comet, tried to drunk-dial Aimee

to verify—who did we end up calling? God?

Some angel told us to accept darkness

and how we laughed as if we'd live

forever. Last year, when you showed me

the waves living under your skin, your muscles

pulsing, we decided you could fight this

and win. We shouted, *We need every spirit*

who can help! and the door blew open.

We were in denial then, trying to avoid your

broken pinecone future. Now we're tucked in

on separate sides of Puget Sound, your world

slighter, mine a body of bees, anxiety is

a tornado circling my life. For years we sailed

together—hasn't everything we've ever loved

been seen from our paddleboards? Our families,

the sunset, the red-wing blackbirds, the book

of poems we left on the sand? The last time

we sailed on the water, we linked our boards

with our paddles, sat side by side and watched

the shore grow smaller. You said I must have

known it was your last paddle, but I saw only

our shadows against the water. My one thought:

This is how we'll stay because we will never end.

MARTHA COLLINS

My Friend

A year ago I failed a good friend for the second time

We have not _______ since

My friend does not _______ me

But tonight I saw my friend in a little box on my computer screen

We did not _______, though people in other boxes _______

The name of our _______ is silence

The name of my friend is _______

Tonight she is all around me, in little boxes

MARTHA COLLINS

From Here

there we are, one of us said,
smoothing the blue sheet

outside the window,
gray trees, bare, except
some oak leaves, clinging

we are here: little arrow pointing

outside, snow falling as rain

over there, everything
gray, falling, except
smoke, then fire rising

little arrows targeting

they are there, some
of them not fallen

SHANTA LEE HONEYCUTT

A Reverse Catechism of How to Take Yourself Back When the World Is Demanding to Eat More Pieces of You *An excerpt*

1. Unsocket, unseat your eyes, see the face that the world will not, won't, isn't allowed to. **2.** Taste yourself upon your own tongue. Do you know your own flavors? **3.** That building… the space wants your body. **4.** Those people, they demand your body   **REFUSE THEM YOUR BODY** (*and you know what they say…don't give breath to that smile, if you can, take your teeth with you, if you can…your whole spirit…DENY THEM*). **5.** If you find yourself in that place or that place with them, with your own bound feet, wrists, and hooded head…kidnap yourself from their laps with necessary violence. **6.** Be the disappeared on your own terms: they don't need to know. **7.** Remain disappeared…you owe them nothing. **8.** Block your ears from the noise… what she say, he say, they say in passing…as help, as advice with tone, all mood, all will with no fucks for you…*careful.* The noise here will deaf and death you. **9.** With full audacity as your birth right because you never apologized for the way you wailed unapologetic when your only language was primal. Sonic. The first lullaby you heard and forgot because of all of the noise. **10.** Go back to the before…

Before there was anything you were ever assigned -
do you remember what it was to just exist like infinity?

Before being dipped in skin inheritance?

Before you knew you were anything separate?
Before you saw your own face to when you just were?

Before you were imprinted with a name, maybe you were in the garden that time that Eve had wisdom to take away such prisons…

Before you were ever standing, walking, running, sitting…back to when you never needed nor asked for any kind of permission to float because time never worked like that there?

We tricked you, those statements posing as questions? you aren't ever given that kinda warning.

And this is why I must tell you. It is written in an ink and alphabet you can't read. In fact I don't need to tell you. You don't need to hear it from the sound of my voice.

Stop listening.
(You already know how to do it….you had it before you came here)

KIM ADDONIZIO

At Twenty

my bed was a mattress on the floor behind a built-in bar
in the basement of a big suburban house, I kept
my textbooks on the shelves, the mattress just fit
between them and the wall, it was cozy, I was studying
French and other subjects, medicating my strep throat
with brown heroin from Mexico, Dave lived across the room
behind a scratched door, making his tortured, meth-induced
impossibly intricate line drawings while my brother
and his friends partied upstairs, I thought I was in love
with a twitchy, guitar-playing junkie named Rabbit,
that was another subject, believing in someone
who'd already given up and gone under
like a diver after a pearl, I was stupid that way
for years, now I want to slap that stupid girl.

KIM ADDONIZIO

As Things Turn Out

The last of the dish soap dies with a wheeze.
Rats peel the rinds from the lemons,
leaving them skinned on the branches.
Onstage, the big soprano pretend-cuts her throat,
then everyone lines up for their coats.
The journalist is shot, then run over.
The king hisses from his swamp.
The princess turns into an ogress.
The prince, relieved, plops back into his pond.
Their children resemble gas masks.
Their grandchildren starve by the truckload
boatload trainload shitload.
Every spring, a few flowers.

DORIANNE LAUX

The Doomsday Clock

"Explain that you live between two great darks, the first

With an ending, the second without one..." -Mark Strand

We're at 100 minutes to midnight.

Where will you be in 100 minutes?

What will you be doing? This morning

I made oatmeal. Five minutes from now

I will probably be washing the pan, the bowl,

my hands in a sink of soapy water

that will drain into a sewer and then

into the sea. See what I mean?

We live so mindlessly, in summer,

through winter, in fall we rake

the dead leaves, in spring, ah

in spring, we sit on the porch and watch

the flowers in their blooming, the bees

at their centers, the birds in the ceramic bath.

It's all I've ever wanted, to be

and to keep being, alive at the pistil,

atop the sticky knob of the stigma, the stalk

or the "style", rising sweetly from the ovary.

Instead I watch TV and the war drones on.

I look up the Extinction Clock,

which is more detailed than the Doomsday Clock

which only measures Nuclear Risk,

Climate Change and Disruptive Technologies

whereas the Extinction Clock tells us

Emperor Penguins could be extinct

in 319 days, that another ice age

could be imminent: 81 days,

that our carbon dioxide budget

will run out in 12 years, but could run out

in as little as 28 days. All depends.

Red wheelbarrow.

White chickens.

DORIANNE LAUX

You

"You
  who the earth was for" --Jean Valentine

Yes, you. This earth, with its prisms
inside the trees, you in your prison
of a mind that won't allow you entry.
You, your family, the bear standing
on two short legs, one clawed paw
deep in a beehive. You who are lost,
wandering the windowless night,
scratching your name in black water,
the purity of stars watching you.
Small, lonely, embarrassed to be alive.
You, open your asthmatic heart, let your
pulse bloom, your face open like a small door.

JENNIFER BARBER
Book Review: *Grief's Apostrophe* by Steven Ratiner
(Beltway Editions, 2025)

The poems in *Grief's Apostrophe* grapple with what the writer of the biblical book
Ecclesiastes formulates as "all that happens under the sun"—times of gladness,
of suffering, of grief—and the meanings to be made of such times over the course
of a life. There are poems about the aging of and subsequent loss of parents;
about grave illness; childhood; the pleasure of ordinary days; and marriage.

Ratiner's poem "We," dedicated to his wife, immerses the reader in its setting,
as the couple roams the beach:

> I walked with you along the sea beside the sea,
> our bare feet disappearing in the sand beneath the sand below the sand.
> Twig-legged plovers scattered before the plovers scattering before us,
> their high-pitched squeaks and skreaks and anxious scurry.

The doubling of the words *sea, plovers,* and *scatter/scattering,* and the tripling in
line two of the word *sand* create moments of dizzying happiness; at the same
time, the writer, like the author of Ecclesiastes, is sharply aware of how fleeting
all moments are:

> We strode until we too shivered into multiplicity—
> our was-is-will-be bleeding one into another. And even when we
> clambered up dune upon wavering dune and, for a moment's moment,
> sat still to gaze, we felt ourselves subsumed within the endless
> succession: blue inside white-pleated undulant blue—
> soul inside sun-anointed rippling soul.

Here too there are strategic repetitions, such as "dune upon wavering dune,"
"a moment's moment" and "soul inside sun-anointed rippling soul"; meanwhile
the "was-is-will-be" contrasts the brief space of a human life against the endless
motion of the seascape.

"Carcinoma," also focuses on the poet and his wife; they were plunged into fear
and uncertainty by her cancer diagnosis, but the outlook improved post-surgery.
The idea of reprieve permeates the poem, which begins,

> Our great good fortune:
> they performed a caesarean

on my wife, extracted death
before it could become full term.

We've given up fear for adoption.
Thank goodness for the days after,

even throbbing with pain, for the day's
repudiation of ever after…

Ratiner uses figurative language to strong effect, equating cancer surgery with a caesarean; the mortal threat is replaced by a kind of rebirth. The couple, having "given the fear up for adoption" instead greet the fragile blessings of the *now*.

It is characteristic of Ratiner's poetry that his vision moves through and beyond his own direct personal experience to encompass what others around him are enduring, as in "Daughter"; I take the "He" to refer to a close friend. These are the first two stanzas:

"That little face…"
He told me it was like
his wife's roses, surrendering
color so slowly they
barely noticed until the morning
the blanched petals lay
scattered beneath the vase.

They brought roses to the hospital
hoping the familiar smell would
remind her, coax her return.
In the silent room,
the plunge and hiss of the breathing machine.
The legato of late afternoon sun.

There is so much sorrow held in the phrase "the legato of late afternoon sun." We learn later in the poem that the child is in a coma. Time itself has been suspended, and the parents have no notion of what the outcome will be. The poem exists as an act of profound empathy.

Empathy and a highly honed poetic sensibility inform Ratiner's weekly online project, Red Letter Poems, where he features recent work by a variety of poets; each poem is accompanied by his insightful and detailed commentary. He is keenly aware of what poems by others achieve, an awareness that funnels into his 2002 book *Giving Their Word: Conversations with Contemporary Poets* (University of Massachusetts Press) and into the architecture of his own poems.

His poem "The Arborist" is a case in point. An elegy for and a tribute to Seamus Heaney, its first section quotes an arborist plunging a steel wand into the ground of the yard as he talks about a root web, "as broad as the dogwood's crown,// feeding the underworld so we here might…/all in good time…." (The ellipses are the author's.)

The arborist's visit gets the poet thinking about burial, and the second section alludes to Heaney's burial in Derry and Psalm 23's phrase "beside the still waters." "That the old text comforted you/is itself a comfort," Ratiner writes, while admitting that he himself is more consoled by Heaney's own "…gravelly syllables tumbled smooth/in the fluency of your voice—the familial//and the forgotten your poetry unearthed."

"The Arborist" concludes with a moving evocation of Heaney's celebrated poem "Digging," which describes the physical labor of Heaney's father and grandfather, compared and contrasted with Heaney's vocation as a writer. The closing lines of "The Arborist" consider the effect Heaney's poetry has had on Ratiner during *his* labor as a writer:

> More than once, it yanked me, despairing, up
>
> from the bog, and back to the work at hand.
> Ineluctable music—even with you gone:
>
> the gruff sound you made cutting turf
> with the nib of your pen—while
>
> your father's fathers bent to their work,
> writing verse with the tips of their spades.

Grief's Apostrophe, too, unearths "the familial and the forgotten." Reading this collection, one encounters the full weight of a life, its suffering and its joys; the poems radiate compassion for others and teach us compassion for ourselves.

CONTRIBUTORS' NOTES

KIM ADDONIZIO has published over a dozen books of poetry and prose. Her most recent poetry collection is *Exit Opera*(W.W. Norton). *Bukowski in a Sundress: Confessions from a Writing Life* was published by Penguin. She has received NEA and Guggenheim Fellowships, Pushcart Prizes in poetry and the essay, and her poetry has been widely translated and anthologized. *Tell Me* was a National Book Award Finalist. She teaches Zoom poetry workshops in Oakland, CA. https://www.kimaddonizio.com

KELLI RUSSELL AGODON is a bi/queer poet from the Pacific Northwest. Her book *Accidental Devotions* will be published by Copper Canyon Press in 2026. Her previous collection, *Dialogues with Rising Tides*, was a finalist for the Washington State Book Awards. Kelli is the cofounder of Two Sylvias Press and teaches in Pacific Lutheran University's MFA program, the Rainier Writing Workshop. She is also the co-host of the poetry series *Poems You Need* with Melissa Studdard. She lives in a seaside town where she is an avid paddleboarder and hiker.

CHRISTOPHER BAKKEN is the author of *Driving the Beast* (LSU Press, 2025) and three previous books of poetry as well as the culinary memoir *Honey, Olives, Octopus: Adventures at the Greek Table*. Twice a Fulbright Scholar, he teaches at Allegheny College and serves as director of Writing Workshops in Greece: Thessaloniki and Thasos.

JENNIFER BARBER's next collection, *A Prevalence of Angels,* will be published by The Word Works in the fall of 2026. She is a co-editor, with Linda Cutting and Tehila Lieberman, of *Blood Moon*, a posthumous collection of poems by Carol Dine (Cervena Barva Press, 2025). Recent poems have appeared in *On the Seawall* and are forthcoming in *Pensive: A Global Journal of Spirituality & the Arts* and in *Plume.*

PICHCHENDA BAO is a Cambodian American writer and poet, infant survivor of the Khmer Rouge regime, daughter of refugees, failed model minority and feminist stay-at-home mother of three. She is one of the co-editors of *Braving the Body* anthology (Harbor Editions). She has received grants, fellowships, and residencies from Queens Council on the Arts, Aspen Words, Kundiman and Bethany Arts Community and serves on the editorial board of Queensbound. More at www.pichchendabao.com.

MILLIE BENSON is an artist based in Brooklyn, New York. Her work has been shown throughout the United States and internationally. Benson moves fluidly between the mediums and methods of composing photographs and collages to an embodied painting practice. Ms. Benson holds a bachelor's degree from the Cleveland Institute of Art and a master's degree in fine arts from Hunter College

ALLISON BLEVINS (she/her) is a queer disabled writer and the author
of *Where Will We Live if the House Burns Down?*, *Cataloguing Pain*, *Handbook for the
Newly Disabled: A Lyric Memoir*, *Slowly/Suddenly*, and six chapbooks. Winner of the
2024 Barthelme Prize, the 2023 Lexi Rudnitsky Editor's Choice Award, and the
2022 Laux/Millar Poetry Prize, Allison serves as the Publisher of Small Harbor
Publishing and lives in Seattle with her spouse and three children.
allisonblevins.com

LEE BRICCETTI is the recipient of a New York Foundation for the Arts
Fellowship for Poetry and a poetry fellowship at the Fine Arts Work Center
in Provincetown. She has been awarded residencies at MacDowell, The
Millay Colony, and the American Academy in Rome. She is the author of *Blue
Guide* (Four Way Books 2018) and *Day Mark* (Four Way Books 2005).

DUSTIN BROOKSHIRE (he/him) is the author of five chapbooks and
the forthcoming full-length collection, *All of Us Faggots* (Iron Oak Editions,
2027). Dustin is the editor of *When I Was Straight: A Tribute to Maureen
Seaton* (Harbor Editions 2024), a 2025 Lambda Literary Award finalist. He is the
co-editor of *Let Me Say This: A Dolly Parton Poetry Anthology* (Madville Publishing,
2023) and can be found online at dustinbrookshire.com.

STEPHANIE BURT is the author of fourteen books of poetry and literary
criticism, including *Super Gay Poems* and *Don't Read Poetry*. A past judge for the
Pulitzer Prize for Poetry, she served as a board member of the National Book
Critics Circle, is the recipient of a Guggenheim Fellowship, and writes regu-
larly for the *New Yorker* and the *London Review of Books*. She is the Donald P. and
Katherine B. Loker Professor of English at Harvard University.

MARY LOU BUSCHI (she/her) authored 3 poetry collections. Her third, *Blue
Physics* (Lily Poetry Review, 2024) was a finalist for Contemporary Poetry in
The International Book Awards and a distinguished favorite for Independent
Press Award. *Paddock* (LPR, 2021) was nominated for The Four Quartets
Prize through The Poetry Society of America. Her poems appear in *Glacier,
Ploughshares, Verse Daily,* among other literary magazines.

PHILIP F. CLARK is the author of *The Carnival of Affection* (Sibling Rivalry
Press, 2018). He received his M.F.A. in Creative Writing in 2016, from
City College (CUNY), New York. The former Poetry Editor of Arts &
Understanding, he has published work in the Tampa Review, Lambda Literary,
and other publications. His work has been included in *On Becoming a Poet* (Marsh
Hawk Press, 2020). He has conducted poetry classes in-person and online for
the Hudson Valley Writers Association.

EILEEN CLEARY is the author of *Wild Pack of the Living* (Nixes Mate
Press,2024), long listed for the Massachusetts Book Award, *2 a.m. with Keats*

(NixesMate Press, 2020) and *Child Ward of the Commonwealth* (Main Street Rag Press, 2019), which received an honorable mention for the Sheila Margaret Motton Book Prize. Her poems have appeared in *Sugar House Review, West Texas Literary Review, The American Journal of Poetry, JAMA, Right Hand Pointing, Verse Daily* and other journals and anthologies. She co-edited the anthology *Voices Amidst the Virus* which was the featured text at the 2021 MSU Filmetry Festival.

MARTHA COLLINS is the author of eleven books of poetry, most recently *Casualty Reports* (Pittsburgh, 2022) and *Because What Else Could I Do* (Pittsburgh, 2019), which won the Poetry Society of America's William Carlos Williams Award. Her fifth volume of co-translated Vietnamese poetry is *Dreaming the Mountain* by Tuệ Sỹ (Milkweed, 2023).

WYN COOPER's sixth book of poems, *The Unraveling*, will be published in May 2026 by White Pine Press. His first novel, *Way Out West* (third printing), is available from Concord Free Press. He has also published five other books of poems: *The Country of Here Below* (Ahsahta Press, 1987), *The Way Back* (White Pine Press, 2000), *Postcards from the Interior,* (BOA Editions, 2005), *Chaos is the New Calm* (BOA Editions, 2010), and *Mars Poetica* (White Pine Press, 2018). His poems, stories, essays, and reviews have appeared in *The New Yorker, The Paris Review, Poetry, Ploughshares, Slate, Crazyhorse, AGNI, The Southern Review,* and more than 100 other magazines. His poems are included in 25 anthologies of contemporary poetry, including *A Century of Poetry in The New Yorker, Poetry: An Introduction (Sixth Edition),* and *The Mercury Reader.*

JESSICA CUELLO's newest book, *Feral*, is forthcoming from JackLeg Press in 2027. Her first volume of translations, *While Percival Fell* by Tania Langlais, a book-length poem about Virginia Woolf's last day, is forthcoming in 2026. Cuello is also the author of *Liar,* selected by Dorianne Laux for The 2020 Barrow Street Book Prize, and three other collections. She is the recipient of a 2025 Saltonstall Fellowship, a 2023 NYSCA Artist Grant, and is poetry editor at *Tahoma Literary Review.* She teaches public school in Central NY..

ROBIN DAVIDSON is a poet and professor emerita of English and creative writing for the University of Houston Downtown. Houston's second poet laureate (2015 - 2017), she is author of two poem chapbooks and two poetry collections, most recently, *Mrs. Schmetterling* (Arrowsmith Press, 2021), and is co-translator with Ewa Elżbieta Nowakowska of two volumes of poems from the Polish of Ewa Lipska, *The New Century* (Northwestern UP, 2009) and *Dear Ms. Schubert* (Princeton UP, 2021).

BRIAN KOMEI DEMPSTER's volumes of poetry, *Seize* (Four Way Books, 2020) and *Topaz* (Four Way Books, 2013), have been selected for various honors, including the Julie Suk Award. He is the editor of *From Our Side of the Fence: Growing Up in America's Concentration Camps* (Kearny Street Workshop, 2001) and

Making Home from War: Stories of Japanese American Exile and Resettlement (Heyday, 2011). He was a 2023 Guggenheim Fellow in Poetry.

PATRICK DONNELLY is the author of five books of poetry, most recently *Willow Hammer* (Four Way Books, 2025). Former poet laureate of Northampton, Massachusetts, Donnelly is program director of The Frost Place, a center for poetry and the arts at Robert Frost's old homestead in Franconia, New Hampshire. His poems have appeared in *American Poetry Review, The Georgia Review, The Iowa Review, The Massachusetts Review, Ploughshares, Slate, The Virginia Quarterly Review, The Yale Review,* and many other journals. Donnelly's translations with Stephen D. Miller of classical Japanese poetry were awarded the 2015-2016 Japan-U.S. Friendship Commission Prize for the Translation of Japanese Literature. Donnelly's other awards include a U.S./Japan Creative Artists Program Award, an Artist Fellowship from the Massachusetts Cultural Council, and an Amy Clampitt Residency Award.

SEAN THOMAS DOUGHERTY's most recent book is *Death Prefers the Minor Keys* from BOA Editions. He works as a third shift long-term Caregiver for folks with traumatic brain injuries in Erie, PA.

DENISE DUHAMEL's most recent books of poetry are *Pink Lady* (Pitt Poetry Series, 2025), *Second Story* (2021) and *Scald* (2017). *Blowout* (2013) was a finalist for the National Book Critics Circle Award. A distinguished university professor in the MFA program at Florida International University in Miami, she lives in Dania Beach.

ALAN FELSENTHAL is the author of *Lowly* (Ugly Duckling Presse, 2017) and *Hereafter* (The Song Cave, 2024). His writing has appeared in *Fence, Harper's, The New York Review of Books,* and *The New York Times Magazine.* He is co-editor of *A Dark Dreambox of Another Kind: The Poems of Alfred Starr Hamilton* and editor of *Bookworm: Conversations with Michael Silverblatt.* He teaches poetry at NYU Tandon School of Engineering.

KATIE FARRIS is the author of the chapbook, *A Net to Catch My Body in its Weaving,* which won the 2020 Chad Walsh Poetry Award, and *boysgirls,* a hybrid-form book. She is also the co-translator of many works from Ukraine, including *The Country Where Everyone's Name is Fear* (Lost Horse Press, 2023), one of *World Literature Today's* Notable Books of 2022. *Standing in the Forest of Being Alive* (Alice James Books, 2023), her debut collection, was shortlisted for the 2023 T.S. Eliot Award.

JENNIFER FRANKLIN is a poet, professor, and editor. She is the author of four poetry collections including *A Fire in Her Brain,* chosen by Rowan Ricardo Phillips for the Princeton Series of Contemporary Poets (Princeton University Press, January 2027). The epistolary poems for Lucia Joyce, Virginia Woolf, and Sylvia Plath from *A Fire in Her Brain* have been published in *American Poetry Review, The Bennington Review, Poetry Northwest, The Montreal International Poetry*

Anthology, the Metropolitan Museum of Art's website, "poem-a-day" on poets. org, *Prairie Schooner,* and The Pushcart Prize Anthology. She is the recipient of a Pushcart Prize, grants from the New York Foundation for the Arts and Café Royal Cultural Foundation, and residencies from Hawthornden Castle in Scotland and the T.S. Eliot House in Gloucester, MA. She teaches in Manhattanville's MFA program, Poets House, The Frost Place, The 92nd St. Y, Provincetown's Fine Arts Work Center & her own manuscript revision workshops. She will be teaching a Master Class for the Kauai Writers Conference in November 2026.

JAN FREEMAN is the author of *Hyena* (Cleveland State University Poetry Center), *Simon Says* (Paris Press/Wesleyan University Press), and *Blue Structure* (Calypso Editions). Her awards include fellowships from MacDowell, the VCCA, and Moulin a Nef. Her poems have appeared in numerous journals, including *APR, Barrow Street, Brooklyn Rail, North American Review, Patterson Review, Plume, Poetry, Salamander,* and *Tar River.* She teaches ekphrastic poetry workshops and directs the MASS MoCA Writing Through Art Poetry Retreats.

SUZANNE FRISCHKORN is the author of four poetry books, most recently *Whipsaw* (Anhinga Press, 2024) a Eugene Paul Nassar Poetry Prize Finalist, as well as five chapbooks. She's the recipient of The Writer's Center Emerging Writers Fellowship for her book, *Lit Windowpane,* the Aldrich Poetry Award for her chapbook *Spring Tide,* selected by Mary Oliver, and a Connecticut Individual Artist Fellowship. Her poems have recently appeared, or are forthcoming in *The Cincinnati Review, Denver Quarterly, North American Review, The Nature of Our Times: Poems on America's Lands, Waters, Wildlife, and Other Natural Wonders,* and *Latino Poetry: A Library of America Anthology.*

BETH GYLYS is the author of five books of poetry and three chapbooks. She is an award-winning author and the co-founder/Principal Investigator of *Beyond Bars: A Journal of Literature and Art,* a Mellon sponsored literary journal for incarcerated writers and artists. Her last two full-length collections (*The Conversation Turns to Wide Mouth Jars*—co-written with Cathy Carlisi and Jennifer Wheelock—and *Body Braille*) were both named Books All Georgians Should Read.

ERICA GOODKIND's poetry, essays, and humor writing have appeared in *The Ekphrastic Review, Capillaries Journal of Medical Humanities, The Fanzine,* and *The Belladonna Comedy.* She holds a B.S. in Nutrition from Bastyr University, a Postbaccalaureate in Creative Writing from the University of Washington, and is currently enrolled in Pacific University's MFA in Poetry program. Erica has enjoyed her work as forest fire lookout, sleep disorders technologist, and gin distillery co-founder. She lives in Seattle.

DAVID GROFF (he/him) is the author of three books of poems, most recently *Live in Suspense,* published by Trio House Press. His previous books are *Clay* and *Theory of Devolution.* He is the coeditor of the anthologies *Who's Yer Daddy?: Gay*

Writers Celebrate Their Mentors and Forerunners and *Persistent Voices: Poetry by Writers Lost to AIDS*. An independent book editor, he teaches in the MFA creative writing program at the City College of New York.

RACHEL HADAS Poet, essayist, and translator Rachel Hadas is the author of many books of poetry, including, most recently, *Pastorals* (2025) from Measure Press and *Ghost Guest* (2023) from Ragged Sky Press. A selection of her essays and criticism, *Piece by Piece*, was published by Paul Dry Books in 2021. Her poem "Voyage" is included in the 2024 edition of The Best American Poetry anthology, edited by Mary Jo Salter.

Hadas is one of some forty translators of the *Dionysiaca* of Nonnus, an epic from late antiquity published by the University Press of Michigan in 2022 as *Tales of Dionysus*; she has also translated three plays by Euripides

Some of her honors include a Guggenheim Fellowship in Poetry, an Ingram Merrill Foundation grant in poetry, and an award in literature from the Academy-Institute of Arts and Letters. She is a recipient of the O.B. Hardison Poetry Prize from the Folger Shakespeare Library.

JARED HARÉL's poetry collection, *Let Our Bodies Change the Subject* (University of Nebraska Press, 2023) was selected by Kwame Dawes as the winner of the Prairie Schooner Raz/Shumaker Book Prize. He's been awarded the 'Stanley Kunitz Memorial Prize' from *American Poetry Review*, the 'William Matthews Prize' from *Asheville Poetry Review*, and his poems have recently appeared in *32 Poems, Ploughshares, Poetry Daily, Southern Review* and *The Sun*. Jared lives with his family in Westchester, NY.

CHARLES O. HARTMAN's most recent collection of poetry is *Downfall of the Straight Line* (Arrowsmith Press, 2024). His other books include *New & Selected Poems* (Ahsahta); a textbook (Verse: An Introduction to Prosody, Wiley-Blackwell); and three books of critical prose (Free Verse, Jazz Text, and Virtual Muse). He co-edited the volume on Wendy Battin for the Unsung Masters series. He is Professor and Poet in Residence Emeritus at Connecticut College. He plays jazz guitar.

JP HOWARD is a poet, educator, literary activist, curator, and community builder. JP was the Spring 2023 Brooklyn College Tow Mentor-in-Residence. Her debut poetry collection, *SAY/MIRROR* (The Operating System), was a Lambda Literary finalist. JP has received fellowships and grants from Cave Canem, VONA, Lambda Literary Foundation, and Brooklyn Arts Council (BAC). She curates Women Writers in Bloom Poetry Salon and her poetry is widely anthologized. JP is a general Poetry Editor for Women's Studies Quarterly and Editor-At-Large of Mom Egg Review VOX online. http://www.jp-howard.com

SHANTA LEE HONEYCUTT is an award-winning visual artist, writer across genres, author, and public intellectual. Winner of the New England Poetry Club's Grant for Poetic Achievement, Abel Meeropol Social Justice Writing Award, and 2024 National Arts Strategies Creative Community Fellow, her work has been widely featured in Harper's Magazine, The Massachusetts Review, Ms. Magazine, DAME Magazine, and elsewhere. She is the author of many collections. her latest work is *Do Words Dream Themselves Into Silence Told In Riddles* (Harbor Editions). Shantalee.com

JENNIFER JEAN is the co-author, with Dr. Hanaa Ahmad, of *Where Do You Live* (Arrowsmith Press, 2025). Her other collections include *VOZ*, *Object Lesson*, and *The Fool*. Her resource book is *Object Lesson: a Guide to Writing Poetry* and she's the editor of the forthcoming anthology *Other Paths of Shahrazad: an Arabic/English Anthology of Contemporary Poetry by Arab Women* (Tupelo Press, 2026). Her work appears in *POETRY Magazine, On the Seawall, The Common, the Los Angeles Review,* on The Slowdown Podcast, and in the Academy of American Poets "Poem-a-Day" series. Jennifer is an organizer for the Her Story Is collective, a faculty member at Solstice MFA, and a senior program manager at the Fine Arts Work Center.

ALLISON JOSEPH is a professor at Southern Illinois University. Her most books include *Dwelling* (Red Hen Press, 2025), *Lexicon* (Red Hen Press, 2021, PBTS Best Book Award winner), and *Confessions of a Barefaced Woman* (Red Hen Press, 2018), winner of the 2019 Feathered Quill Book Award and a finalist for the 2019 NAACP Image Award. She was named Illinois Author of the Year for 2022 by the Illinois Association of Teachers of English. Her poems have appeared in the *New York Times* and in the *Best American Poetry*. She is the widow of beloved poet and editor Jon Tribble. She lives in Carbondale, Illinois.

AMY KING is the author of *The Missing Museum* (Tarpaulin Sky, 2026) and *I Want to Make You Safe* (Litmus Press, 2011). King was the recipient of the 2015 Winner of the WNBA Award (Women's National Book Association). She serves on the executive board of VIDA: Women in Literary Arts and co-edited with Heidi Lynn Staples the anthology, *Big Energy Poets of the Anthropocene: When Ecopoets Think Climate Change*. She is an Associate Professor of Creative Writing at SUNY Nassau Community College.

STEPH KLEID (she/her) is a New Jersey-based poet and writer. She received her BA and MFA in Creative Writing from Manhattanville University, where she is now an academic writing lecturer. Her work can be found in *Sinking City, Creation Magazine,* and *Sugared Water* by Porkbelly Press. Steph is drawn to narrative poetry and stories that explore femininity, the body, and love in its many forms.

DORIANNE LAUX Pulitzer Prize finalist Dorianne Laux's *Only As the Day is Long: New and Selected Poems* is available from W.W. Norton as are her award winning books, *Facts about the Moon* and *The Book of Men*. A text book, *Finger Exercises for Poets*, is just out from as well as, *Life on Earth*, poems. She is founding faculty at Pacific University's Low Residency MFA and a chancellor of The Academy of American Poets. https://www.doriannelaux.net/

ESTHER LIN (she/her) was born in Rio de Janeiro, Brazil, and lived in the United States as an undocumented immigrant for 21 years. She is the author of *Cold Thief Place* (Alice James, 2025), which was longlisted for the National Book Award, and co-editor of *Here to Stay: Poetry and Prose from the Undocumented Diaspora* (HarperCollins, 2024). She won a 2024 Pushcart Prize and is a former Wallace Stegner Fellow.

KATE MACLAUCHLAN's work examines familial relationships and growing up queer in the rural south. She explores themes of guilt and displacement, often through the lens of the Icarus myth. Her poems can be found in *The Marbled Sigh Journal, Pink Apple Press, Chaotic Merge Magazine, and OnGaia Literary Magazine.*

CYNTHIA MANICK is the author of *No Sweet Without Brine* (Amistad-HarperCollins, 2023), which received 5 stars from Roxane Gay, was named among the "Best Poetry of the Last Year" by *Ms. Magazine,* and was selected as a New York Public Library Best Book of 2023. She is the author of *Brown Girl Polaris* (a Belladonna chaplet), editor of *The Future of Black: Afrofuturism, Black Comics, and Superhero Poetry;* and winner of the Lascaux Prize in Collected Poetry for her first collection *Blue Hallelujahs.* Manick has received fellowships from Cave Canem, Hedgebrook, MacDowell, Yaddo, and Château de la Napoule among other foundations. She lives in New York, but travels widely for poetry.

FRED MARCHANT is the author of five books of poetry, the most recent of which is *Said Not Said,* (Graywolf Press). Marchant is also editor of *Another World Instead,* early poems by William Stafford, and co-editor of *Tree Lines,* poems about trees and forests. His poetry is found in various anthologies, including *Braving the Body* (Small Harbor). Marchant has new work in journals such as *Arrowsmith, The New Yorker, Solstice,* and *Plume.*

DANA HENRY MARTIN is a poet, weaver, and musician who advocates for humane, holistic health- and mental-health care and LGBTQIA+ rights. Martin's chapbooks include *Love and Cruelty* (Meat for Tea, forthcoming), *No Sea Here* (Moon in the Rye Press, forthcoming), *Toward What Is Awful* (YesYes Books), *In the Space Where I Was* (Hyacinth Girl Press), and *The Spare Room* (Blood Pudding Press).

JENNIFER MARTELLI (1962-2025) authored four chapbooks and four full-length poetry collections including *Psychic Party Under the Bottle Tree* (2024, Lily Poetry Review Books) which was longlisted for the Massachusetts Book Award and *The Queen of Queens* (Bordighera Press) which won the Italian American Studies Association Book Award and was shortlisted for the Massachusetts Book Award. Her work has been published in The Academy of American Poets *Poem-A-Day, Poetry, Best of the Net Anthology, Braving the Body Anthology, Verse Daily, Plume, The Tahoma Literary Review*, and elsewhere. She received fellowships from The Virginia Center for the Creative Arts, Monson Arts, and the Massachusetts Cultural Council. She served as the poetry co-editor of MER.

LYNN MCGEE 's most recent poetry collection is *Science Says Yes* (Broadstone Books, 2024). Her other collections include *Tracks* (Broadstone Books, 2019) and *Sober Cooking* (Spuyten Duyvil Press, 2016), as well as two award-winning poetry chapbooks: *Heirloom Bulldog* (Bright Hill Press, 2015) and *Bonanza* (SHP, 1997). Her poems have appeared in *Slant, San Pedro River Review, North Dakota Quarterly, Naugatuck River Review, Sugar House Review, Lascaux Review, The Atlanta Review, Atticus Review, Tampa Review,* and *Sugar House Review.*

PHILIP MEMMER is the author of six books of poems, most recently *Cairns* (Lost Horse Press, 2022). His work has appeared in such journals as *Poetry* and *Poetry London,* in many anthologies, and in the Library of Congress's "Poetry 180" website. He lives in upstate New York, where he founded and directs the YMCA's Downtown Writers Center in Syracuse, serves as Publisher at Tiger Bark Press, and teaches at Hamilton College.

JENNIFER MILITELLO is the Poet Laureate of New Hampshire. She is the author of the hybrid collection *Identifying the Pathogen* (Tupelo Press, 2026), named a finalist for the FC2 Ronald Sukenick Innovative Fiction Prize, the memoir *Knock Wood* winner of the Dzanc Nonfiction Prize, and five collections of poetry, including, most recently, *The Pact* (TupeloPress/Shearsman Books, 2021). She teaches in the MFA program at New England College.

CARIDAD MORO-GRONLIER In 2024, Caridad Moro-Gronlier became Miami-Dade County's first woman and second Poet Laureate. Author of *Visionware* (FLP 2009), *Tortillera* (TRP, 2021), *Through the Lens* (2026), and editor of *Grabbed* (Beacon Press, 2020), in 2025 she served as a National Book Award poetry judge and an Academy of American Poets Poet Laureate Fellow. She's Senior Editor for SWWIM and Poetry Curator at The Betsy Hotel. Her work appears in *NPR, The Slowdown,* and more. She lives in Miami, FL

D. NURKSE is the author of twelve books of poetry, most recently, *A Country of Strangers: New and Selected Poems* (Knopf, 2022). His many honors include a Literature Award from the American Academy of Arts and Letters and a Guggenheim Fellowship. His poems have appeared in *The New Yorker, The American Poetry Review,* and *The Paris Review.* He has taught poetry in prison, and, as Brooklyn poet laureate, in local schools and the public library system. A resident of Brooklyn, he currently teaches in the MFA program at Sarah Lawrence College.

ALICIA OSTRIKER has published nineteen collections of poetry, been twice nominated for the National Book Award, and has twice received the National Jewish Book Award for Poetry, among other honors. Her most recent poetry collections are *The Volcano Sequence and After: Selected and New Poems 2002-2019* and *The Holy and Broken Bliss: Poems in Plague Time.* She was New York State Poet Laureate 2018-2021.

E.K. PIGNOTTI is an undergraduate creative writing and theatre major in New York. They are 19 years old, born in Chicago, Illinois. They write short stories, poems, and plays.

IAIN HALEY POLLOCK is the author of three poetry collections, most recently, *All the Possible Bodies* (Alice James Books, 2025). His poems have appeared in numerous publications including *American Poetry Review, The New York Times Magazine,* and *The Progressive.* Pollock has received several honors for his work including the Cave Canem Poetry Prize, the Alice Faye di Castagnola Award from the Poetry Society of America, and a nomination for an NAACP Image Award. He serves as Director of the MFA Program in Creative Writing at Manhattanville University.

CONNIE POST served as Poet Laureate of Livermore, California (2005-2009). Her work has appeared in *Calyx, Cutthroat, River Styx, Slipstream, Spoon River Poetry Review,* & *Valparaiso Poetry Review.* Her awards include the Crab Creek Poetry Prize, Liakoura Award and the Caesura Poetry Award.. Her second full length book, *Prime Meridian* was released in January 2020 (Glass Lyre Press) and was a finalist for the 2020 Best Book Awards. Her most recent books are *Between Twilight* from New York Quarterly Books and *Broken Metronome* from Glass Lyre Press. *Broken Metronome* was the winner of the American Fiction Award for poetry chapbook.

PIA QUINTANO is a New York based writer and painter who often suggests narratives with her artwork. Her paintings were sold at the Frank J. Miele Contemporary American Folk Art Gallery in NYC until it closed. Her artwork has appeared in *Glass Mountain, Peatsmoke, Saranac Review, Emerson Review, Red Ogre,* and *Harpur Palate,* among other journals. She shares a cozy apartment near the park with a small menagerie and many plants.

GRACE SCHULMAN received the Frost Medal for Distinguished Lifetime Achievement in American Poetry, and is a member of The American Academy of Arts and Letters. She is the author of nine books of poems, including *Again, the Dawn: New and Selected Poems, 1976-2022.* Other books include a memoir, *Strange Paradise: Portrait of a Marriage,* and an essay collection, *First Loves and Other Adventures.* Editor of *The Poems of Marianne Moore,* she is Distinguished Professor Emerita at Baruch College, C.U.N.Y., formerly Poetry Editor of *The Nation* and Director, Poetry Center, 92Y. Her honors include a Guggenheim Fellowship and six Pushcart Prizes.

JOANNA SOLFRIAN is the author of the poetry collections *Temporary Beast, The Second Perfect Number, The Mud Room,* and *Visible Heavens,* which was chosen by Naomi Shihab Nye for the Wick First Book Poetry Prize. Her poems have appeared in *The Harvard Review, Boulevard, Rattle, Margie, The Southern Review, Salamander, Pleiades, Image,* and elsewhere. She is a MacDowell Fellow and a five-time Pushcart nominee. Joanna lives and works in New York City. www.joannasolfrian.com

PAGE HILL STARZINGER's second book, *Vortex Street* (2020), was short-listed for the Grand Prize in Poetry by the Eric Hoffer Award Committee. Her first book, *Vestigial* (2013), won the Barrow Street Book Prize, selected by Lynn Emanuel. Both, Barrow Street Press. Her chapbook, *Unshelter* (2009), won the Noemi Chapbook Contest, chosen by Mary Jo Bang. Poems are forthcoming or have appeared in *The New Yorker, Revel, American Poetry Review, Kenyon Review, Volt,* and others.

LINDA STORM With her paintings and installations, Linda Storm stirs wonder by her depictions of nature, and myths. Her art is exhibited and collected around the world and licensed for publications, album covers, stage projections, and murals. Linda is an alumni of Chateau Orquevaux Art Residency, France, a member of the National Museum of Women Artists, represented by Singulart Gallery, and a juried member of the esteemed National Association of Women Artists. Find more at LindaStormArt.com

YERRA SUGARMAN's three volumes of poetry are: *Aunt Bird* (Four Way Books, 2022), which won American Book Fest's 2022 Best Book Award for General Poetry, and was a finalist for the National Jewish Book Award in Poetry; *The Bag of Broken Glass* (Sheep Meadow, 2008), poems from which received a National Endowment for the Arts Fellowship; and *Forms of Gone* (Sheep Meadow, 2002), winner of PEN American Center's Joyce Osterweil Award for Poetry.

LISA J. SULLIVAN holds an MFA in Poetry from the Solstice MFA in Creative Writing Program, where she was a Kurt Brown Memorial Fellow. Her poems, book reviews, and artist interviews have appeared in *The Comstock Review, Burningword Literary Journal, The Chaffin Journal, Evening Street Review,* and elsewhere. She was the United States winner of The Poetry Project–Ireland in collaboration with the Academy of American Poets and was an Adrian Tinsley Program Creative Grant recipient. Lisa is the Art Editor for *Lily Poetry Review* and a Poetry Editor for *Pink Panther Magazine.* Her debut poetry collection *Theory of Impact* is forthcoming from Lily Poetry Review Press.

HEATHER TRESELER is author of *Auguries & Divinations,* which received the 2025 Massachusetts Book Award in poetry, and the chapbooks *Hard Bargain* and *Parturition.* Her poems have received a Pushcart Prize, the W. B. Yeats Prize, and *Narrative Magazine's* poetry prize and appear in *Harvard Review,*

The Iowa Review and *The Irish Times*. She is professor of English at Worcester State University and a scholar at the Brandeis Women's Studies Research Center.

MICHAEL TYRELL is a poet, actor, visual artist, and professor. He is the author of *The Wanted* (National Poetry Review, 2012) *Phantom Laundry* (Backlash, 2017), and *The Arsonist's Letters* (Backlash, 2021). With Julia Spicher Kasdorf, he edited *Broken Land: Poems of Brooklyn* (NYU Press, 2007). His poems have appeared in *Agni, The Best American Poetry, The Iowa Review, The Paris Review, Ploughshares, The Yale Review*, and many other publications. A native of Brooklyn, he teaches at New York University.

BARBARA UNGAR's sixth book, *After Naming the Animals*, addressing the sixth extinction, appeared in 2024 from The Word Works, which also published *Immortal Medusa and Charlotte Brontë, You Ruined My Life*. Earlier books include *Save Our Ship*, which won the Snyder Prize from Ashland Poetry Press, and *The Origin of the Milky Way*, which won the Gival Poetry Prize. She has published in *Scientific American, Salmagundi, The Southern Indiana Review, Pedestal*, and many other journals.

PETER URKOWITZ lives in Salem, Massachusetts, where he works in a college library. He was drawn to the local poetry scene as a spectator and began writing his own work. He has published poems in *Meat for Tea: The Valley Review* and in *Oddball Magazine*. He is the author of *Fake Zodiac Signs: An Astro-Illogical Guidebook*.

JESSICA L. WALSH's latest book is *Blowdown* (Small Harbor, 2026). She is also the author of *Book of Gods and Grudges* (Glass Lyre, 2022) as well as two previous collections, *The List of Last Tries* and H*ow to Break My Neck*. Her work has appeared on the Best American Poetry Blog and journals like *Painted Bride Quarterly, RHINO, Indianapolis Review, Crab Creek Review*, and more. Her poetry has won multiple editorial prizes and has been nominated several times for the Pushcart Prize, Best New Poets, and Best of the Net. She received a BA from Kalamazoo College and a PhD from University of Iowa. Originally from small-town Michigan, she currently lives outside of Chicago and teaches at a community college.

ANTHONY WALTON's poems have appeared in *The New Yorker, The American Scholar, The American Academy of Poets, The Black Scholar, Poetry Ireland*, and *The Library of America*. A celebrated author of non-fiction, his books include *Mississippi, The End of Respectability*, and, with Michael S. Harper, *The Vintage Anthology of African American Poetry*. A chapbook, *1968*, recently appeared, and his first collection, *Celestial Mechanics*, will appear in the fall from Godine.

WILLIAM WEBB lives in Berkeley, California. He is a Faculty Associate and is on the Advisory Board of the *Institute of Writing and Thinking* at Bard College.

He is a writer, a cook, a painter and a swimmer. He and his husband and their dog Turnip can often be found in the hills walking or on the couch reading. He has published in print and online journals including, *Field Notes, La Voz, the NAIS Magazine, Anthem, Nixes Mate Review* and in the upcoming book, *The Work of Jobs: Poems about Work.*

AMIE WHITTEMORE (she/her) is the author of four poetry collections, most recently the chapbook *Hesitation Waltz* (Midwest Writing Center). She was the 2020-2021 Poet Laureate of Murfreesboro, Tennessee, and an Academy of American Poets Laureate Fellow. Her poems have won multiple awards, including a Dorothy Sargent Rosenberg Prize, and her writing has appeared in *Blackbird, Colorado Review, Terrain.org, Pleiades,* and elsewhere. She teaches creative writing at Eastern Illinois University.

JUSTIN WYMER is a poet, nonfiction and cross-genre writer and educator. Born and raised in southwestern West Virginia, he holds degrees from Harvard University; the Iowa Writers' Workshop; and the University of Denver, where he studied creative writing and literary arts with a focus on trauma studies, queer stylistics, and literature of excess and difficulty. Wymer's debut full-length collection, *Deed,* won the 2018 Antivenom Poetry Award and was published by Elixir Press in 2019. His second poetry collection, *Let the Forest Go: Poems,* is forthcoming from University Press of Kentucky in June 2026. He lives and teaches in Tennessee.

ANTON YAKOVLEV full-length poetry collection *One Night We Will No Longer Bear the Ocean* came out in June 2024 from Redacted Books (ELJ Editions). His most recent chapbook *Chronos Dines Alone* (SurVision Books, 2018) won the James Tate Prize. His poems have appeared in *The New Yorker, Poetry Daily, The Hopkins Review, Crab Orchard Review, Plume, upstreet,* and elsewhere. Anton is a former education director at Bowery Poetry Club.

ZAHRA ZOGHI (she/her) is a multi-disciplinary artist based in Tehran with over three decades of experience. Her work explores themes of memory, identity, and transformation through richly textured surfaces, emotional abstraction, and symbolic bird imagery. Her art has been featured on covers and within numerous literary magazines across North America and Europe. She holds a Master's in Art Research and mentors emerging artists. Her visual language honors tradition while inviting new ways of seeing.